UNITED STATES
FOREIGN POLICY

UNITED STATES FOREIGN POLICY

ITS ORGANIZATION AND CONTROL

Report
OF A STUDY GROUP FOR THE
WOODROW WILSON FOUNDATION, Study group,
.. 1950-51.

WILLIAM YANDELL ELLIOTT
CHAIRMAN OF THE STUDY GROUP

Preface
BY HARRY D. GIDEONSE
PRESIDENT, WOODROW WILSON FOUNDATION

COLUMBIA UNIVERSITY PRESS, NEW YORK

First printing 1952
Second printing 1953

This is the report of the first of a series of Study
Groups set up by the Woodrow Wilson Foundation for study and research directed toward the
problem of how the structure and practices of
our government might be improved to permit the
full and effective discharge of American responsibilities and obligations in interrelated domestic
and international affairs and the stimulation of
popular thinking along these lines.

PUBLISHED IN GREAT BRITAIN, CANADA, INDIA, AND PAKISTAN
BY GEOFFREY CUMBERLEGE: OXFORD UNIVERSITY PRESS
LONDON, TORONTO, BOMBAY, AND KARACHI
MANUFACTURED IN THE UNITED STATES OF AMERICA

MEMBERS OF THE STUDY GROUP

WILLIAM YANDELL ELLIOTT, CHAIRMAN
WILLIAMS PROFESSOR OF HISTORY AND POLITICAL SCIENCE
HARVARD UNIVERSITY

McGEORGE BUNDY
ASSOCIATE PROFESSOR OF GOVERNMENT
HARVARD UNIVERSITY

HARRY D. GIDEONSE
PRESIDENT OF BROOKLYN COLLEGE, NEW YORK

GEORGE F. KENNAN
FOREIGN SERVICE OFFICER ON LEAVE OF ABSENCE
AT INSTITUTE FOR ADVANCED STUDY
PRINCETON, NEW JERSEY

DON K. PRICE
ASSOCIATE DIRECTOR, PUBLIC ADMINISTRATION CLEARING HOUSE
WASHINGTON, D.C.

ARTHUR M. SCHLESINGER, JR.
ASSOCIATE PROFESSOR OF AMERICAN HISTORY
HARVARD UNIVERSITY

PREFACE

IN THE SPRING of 1950 the Woodrow Wilson Foundation authorized the selection and designation of a Study Group to engage in study and research on the problem of how the structure and practices of our government might be improved to permit the full and effective discharge of American responsibilities and obligations in interrelated domestic and international affairs and the stimulation of popular thinking along these lines. In accordance with the Board's decision, the President of the Foundation sought and secured the services of Dr. William Y. Elliott as chairman of the Study Group for the year 1950–51, and it was possible to arrange for the initial meeting of the Group as a whole in August, 1950.

Since we began with the objective of securing as much diversity of viewpoint and experience as was compatible with an interest in the selected topic, as well as demonstrated capacity for the give-and-take of a group project, we anticipated some difficulty in the composition of the Study Group, especially in view of the Board's additional concern for representation including scholarship about the past as well as a reflection of more recent experience in actual administration. It is probably a sign that the Foundation has decided to develop a field that has "high priority" in the minds of qualified students of our government that we secured the consent to serve of every member of our "first-choice" team—and that a planning meeting was possible in the middle of the summer of 1950 to prepare for the work of the coming year.

The Study Group, which has met regularly during the past year, has consisted of the following members—apart from the President of the Foundation, who served as a member at Dr. Elliott's as well as the Board's request:

William Y. Elliott—*Chairman*

    Williams Professor of History and Political Science, Harvard University

    Author: *The Pragmatic Revolt in Politics; The New British Empire; The Need for Constitutional Reform; Western Political Heritage; Colmer and Herter Committee Reports on Foreign Aid* (House of Representatives) and *Senate Document* 204, 81st Congress: 2nd Session; and various studies on mobilization and security planning

    Sometime Vice Chairman for Civilian Requirements, War Production Board, and Staff Director, Herter Committee (House of Representatives) and Foreign Affairs Committee (House of Representatives) 80th Congress

    Special Assistant to the Director, Office of Defense Mobilization

McGeorge Bundy

    Associate Professor of Government, Harvard University

    Joint author with Henry L. Stimson: *On Active Service in Peace and War*

    Editor: *The Pattern of Responsibility*

George F. Kennan

    American Foreign Service Officer, since 1926; currently on leave-of-absence at Institute for Advanced Study, Princeton, New Jersey

    Formerly, Deputy for Foreign Affairs, National War College (1946–47)

    Director, Policy Planning Staff, Department of State (1947–49)

    Counselor of Department of State (1949–50)

    Author: *American Diplomacy, 1900–1950*

Don K. Price

Associate Director, Public Administration Clearing House

Board of Directors, Social Science Research Council
Formerly Assistant to former President Hoover for the study of
the Presidency under the Commission on Organization of the
Executive Branch of the Government (1948–1949)
Formerly Staff Member, United States Bureau of the Budget
(1945–1946)

Arthur M. Schlesinger, Jr.

Associate Professor of American History, Harvard University
Author: *The Age of Jackson; The Vital Center; The General and
the President* (with R. H. Rovere)

In addition, Dr. Frances R. Fussell has served as rapporteur
and editorial assistant to the chairman. She was formerly a
member of the Department of Political Science at Swarthmore
College, a member of the staff of the War Production Board
(1941–45), the Department of State (1945–49), and the Joint
Congressional Committee on Foreign Economic Policy (1948–
49).

The Study Group has had the benefit of consultation with
qualified students of its problem, including Elmer Davis,
Lincoln Gordon, Ernest A. Gross, Colonel G. R. Lincoln, C. B.
Marshall, Arthur W. McMahon, and Reinhold Niebuhr. In
many cases monographs on special topics which were written
by members of the Study Group were submitted for critical
discussion by these consultants, as well as by the Study Group
as a whole. None of these consultants is responsible for any
of the text or conclusions in the final report.

The purposes of this Study on "United States Foreign Policy:
Its Organization and Control" were twofold:

(1) To stimulate academic interest in the political theory
and practice of United States foreign policy, and to
provide government practitioners with useful signposts
for improvement in the conduct of foreign affairs

(2) To select, for recommended research, general problems
and specific illustrations where further studies would
be most useful contributions both to theoretical knowledge and to the practice of government

The Study analyzes some of the modern problems in the
organizational formation and control of United States foreign
policy that arise from the basic structure of the government
in its historical, constitutional, economic, political, and military
aspects. This involved casting up discrepancies in theory and
practice resulting from the complications of the interrelationship of the Executive and the Legislature. It called for an
assessment of short-term domestic political factors against
long-term national interest. It dealt with the interplay of
economics, politics, and military strategy on the constitutional
prerogatives of checks and balances. It took into account the
interaction of federal government with international government at the point of foreign and military policy. Although the
emphasis of the Study is on problems posed for American
political analysis, it is hoped that it will also be useful to
government practitioners in improving the conduct of United
States foreign policy, and to the layman in understanding better its basic imperatives.

While this particular report touches upon the life and writings of Woodrow Wilson only in passing, the Study Group was
conscious of the debt that American political theory owes to
the man whose name this Foundation bears.

Historical research in the organizational aspects of foreign
policy problems as they presented themselves to Woodrow
Wilson would be of particular interest, if space were available,
for reasons other than a proper loyalty to the Foundation.

In the first place, Woodrow Wilson was himself a considerable political theorist; and although he came to his pre-
dominant interest in foreign policy and world organization late

in life, he had laid a substantial groundwork in five other aspects of his own development:

(a) He was, among other things, a deep student of international law and a strong exponent of a juristic basis for relations between States. One sees a great deal of the Germanic influence in this aspect of Wilson's thinking; whereas in other fields of political analysis his debt was to British and American historical study, to Bagehot in particular.

(b) He was a historian of great parts in his own right. The bulk of his writing in this field is not considerable unless one includes as historical, in the best sense, his works on *Constitutional Government* and *Congressional Government*. But there shines through all his Presidential Papers and Addresses, as well as in his *Mere Literature and Other Essays,* a deep sense of the best historical tradition—that is, the *re*-creation of the whole feeling of periods of the past and their interpretation in terms of the living present.

(c) In his really outstanding works on *Constitutional Government* and *Congressional Government,* Woodrow Wilson made the most systematic analysis of the functioning of the American political system that possibly any single American political writer has accomplished. His deep insights can be judged by the brief excerpts on the issues relevant to the whole topic of inquiry of the Study Group. For purposes of analysis, it should be noted that *Congressional Government,* which he wrote as a theorist without practical experience, raised the crucial issue now before the American people—namely, the effect of the separation of powers and the possibility under American conditions of improving the operation of this system.

Few people have better understood the dynamics of parties and representative institutions, both legislative and executive. At the same time, Wilson presents "the great tradition." He faced the dilemma of organizing power adequately yet main-

taining the moral restraints of fundamental law. Few writers
have been more conscious of the difficulties which the complex
balancing of objectives imposed upon political leadership in
the United States.

Wilson, better than any of his contemporaries, understood
that democracy could destroy itself by relying on the romantic
view that the will of the people could be translated into action
automatically by the electoral process. He knew that moral
enthusiasm and indignation were not enough. That led him
to his leadership in the "short ballot" movement and to his
stimulation of American interest in the improvement of administration.

(d) Throughout the whole of Woodrow Wilson's public life
and academic reflections ran the idea of greater executive
responsibility for greater cooperation with the legislatures at
the local, state, national, and international levels, in order to
simplify the mechanics of American government. This was—
and is—particularly important at the national level, where
foreign policy has come to represent the greatest strain on the
American system.

(e) Finally, it was Woodrow Wilson himself who offered
an example at once dramatically successful and, in the end,
tragic of the working of political leadership in evolving the
first stages of a mature American foreign policy to a position of
world leadership. It was he who rallied the imagination of the
entire Western World and penetrated even the Orient with
the "magic" of his Fourteen Points. It was he who in the end
was broken, perhaps as much by the strain of the Presidency
and the conflicting pulls which it imposed as by the failure of
the Senate to ratify the Treaty of Versailles. With this failure
the possibility of a vital League of Nations also perished. In
the life and works of Woodrow Wilson can be seen the great
historic preamble to the continuing modern problem which this

country has had to face in its search for an adequate system for the formation and control of foreign policy.

This Study, however, is not aimed at the ideas of Woodrow Wilson, illuminating and apt as they are. It tries to assess the nature of the American political process as a whole as it bears on foreign policy. It is not a purely descriptive study nor a merely clinical analysis. It adopts the bolder values: to prescribe and to suggest remedies. Perhaps this effort flies in the everyday face of the present academic tradition of this nation. But it is true to the great tradition of the founders of the nation, of the authors of the *Federalist,* and of the men who not only made but gave living shape to the new Constitution. The effort, at least, is worthy of the inspiration of Woodrow Wilson.

The members of the Study Group have authorized me to include in this preface a statement as to the methods by which this Study was prepared. Diffuse statement is characteristic of any group effort. In the very nature of the enterprise, it is difficult, if not impossible, to arrive at a precipitate of the group's discussions that would be acceptable in all its specific details to every individual member of the group. This would apply to Dr. William Y. Elliott, the chairman of the Group, who served as the rapporteur, as much as to the other members. We have made a deliberate effort, however, to state the issues and the conclusions clearly, and we have sought to avoid watering down every formulation to a common denominator. This means that there is some possibility of dissent by one member or another on almost every page. The final formulation represents a fair exposition of the consensus of the Study Group as to the points on which the discussion turned as well as a clear indication of the points on which there was disagreement. We have added as Appendix II a series of brief statements by individual members of the Study Group on the points of substance or emphasis on which they found themselves in some measure of disagreement with the consensus of the Group's views.

The object of the Study was to stimulate further research and to point up the issues which seemed to be most worthy of further development. They represent a unique consensus among a strong group of qualified minds. There are issues and alternatives in policy on which it is not reasonable to expect complete agreement, but if its authors have been able to transmit some of the clarification of basic issues which they experienced themselves in its preparation, the Study will have achieved its primary objective.

HARRY D. GIDEONSE
President, Woodrow Wilson Foundation

January 15, 1952

CONTENTS

PART II

The Ultimate Control in a Democracy

PART III

Power, Principle, and Policy

PART IV

Summary of Suggestions and Conclusions

APPENDICES

INTRODUCTION

I

INTRODUCTION

D URING the past few years many people have had a feeling
of more than normal frustration about the conduct of
international affairs. As complications and new dangers
have grown well-nigh incredible and, to some simply unbear-
able, the old techniques and rules of conduct no longer seem to
apply. Some of this feeling may be due to atomic jitters and
to a state of general anger or shock produced by Moscow's
aims and tactics. But much of the difficulty comes from the
fact that we can no longer delude ourselves into thinking that
foreign policy is something separate and apart. It is now so
thoroughly intermingled with domestic affairs that we can no
longer make decisions on what we have always thought of as
just our own affairs. We are always running into the world
effects of our own politics or, conversely, the domestic reper-
cussions of world commitments by the United States.

All this forces us to come to new ideas about our national
interest and our foreign policy—neither simple nor easy of
solution: Is food for India foreign policy? Then so is the wheat
supply, and parity payments, and soil conservation, and whatever the Dakota farmer may think of all these things. Is the
supply of arms to the North Atlantic Treaty nations foreign
policy? Then so is the manufacture of steel and the amorti-
zation of taxes on new plants, price control and allocation
policy, and the ideas of the National Association of Manufacturers and the Congress of Industrial Organizations. Is our

national interest bound up with the fate of Europe to such a degree that we must not get out of step with France, England, and the rest? Where does this dependence stop? How can we combine American politics and this sort of world "leadership"?

It is intensely irritating to Americans (as it has no doubt been for centuries to Europeans, now grown hardened to the facts) that foreign policy is not just a "unilateral" affair. Foreign policy must, even for a powerful nation, mean accommodation of national policy to the desires and power of other nations—factors beyond our own control.

We are forced to observe, in a hazy and often reluctant way, that all parts of our own society are affected by world affairs. We are sometimes embarrassed, also, to discover in specific instances that almost every department of the federal government has control over some action crucial to our international relations and, worse still, that each department seems at times determined to go its own way regardless of the rest. Then we wake up to realize that the United States government has taken on world-wide responsibilities before it has learned to organize its own affairs in a disciplined and responsible manner. For it is not only administrative rationalizing of policy that is in question; it is our whole rather easy-going process of politics by pressure and adjustment.

It is no wonder that this is distressing to the most able men America has trained in the business of foreign affairs. The American diplomat abroad understood the line of communication back to the Secretary of State and the President. He understood the line to the foreign government that had received his credentials. He was beginning to understand the concept of international organization and the lines that today run to the United Nations. But the picture began to be complicated to a unique degree by a fourth factor—the lines of coordination within the United States government itself. Congress, under the impact of the new forces, began to demand as much of his diplomacy as did the foreign governments and people with whom he had habitually dealt. This was made manifest in the flesh by a legion of legislators on "study tours," covering our foreign missions like a blanket.

Can the government of the United States speak with a single voice in world affairs? Or will our internal irresponsibility cancel out our great power? Can we make a promise to the world and then "deliver the goods?" On the other hand, can foreign nations play off one part of our government against another? Worse still, will we project our internal divisions on the outside world? Will the contradictions in our national policy stir up dissensions among the free nations?

What Montesquieu has called "the spirit of laws" is especially evident in the conduct of a nation's foreign policy. This "spirit" is discernible in the operation of a nation's constitutional system, in the protection of its civil liberties, and in the broad outlines of its representative machinery. But since the very life of the nation today depends upon the success of its foreign policy, it is in the formation and conduct of this area of policy that a political system most reveals its inner essence. Its weaknesses here may be fatal. How may we summarize our own national experience?

From George Washington to John Quincy Adams, the Executive clearly took the dominant part in the development of United States foreign policy. Yet the way of executive policies in Congress was hardly a smooth one. In this period, when the United States still seemed intimately involved in European power conflicts and before it had become fully committed to westward expansion, foreign policy was inevitably of vital concern to the nation. It was a great issue in party rivalry, with echoes in Congress and the nation.

In the generation after the War of 1812, Americans began to shift their attention inward. Foreign affairs had a decreasing pressure behind them. The very concept of "national interests" receded into a dim background; the function of foreign policy seemed increasingly to be the protection abroad of the individual interests (generally commercial) of United States citizens. The absence of an executive foreign policy created a vacuum into which Congress irresistibly advanced. No great harm was done, perhaps, by the incursion, since national interest was so narrowly involved.

In the period after the Civil War, Congress asserted its power so ruthlessly through the treaty veto that some observers came to feel that a positive foreign policy was no longer possible under our system because of what one Secretary of State called the "irreparable mistake of the Constitution."

Yet as its industrial power increased, the United States was bound to play an ever larger part in the world political arena. Thus, around the turn of the century, foreign policy acquired a new urgency—a change dramatically signalized by the Spanish-American War.

With the accession of Theodore Roosevelt to the Presidency there began one more reversal of the balance of power, the Executive acquiring new authority and tending increasingly to by-pass Congress.

Wilson's period continued this trend but showed that Congress must be carried along. The rejection of the Treaty of Versailles administered a check to these tendencies, and Congress sought to reassert its claim in the quiet period of the twenties.

With the thirties, foreign policy once more became critical; and once more the result was an increase in the power of the President. Continued crises after the second World War have thrust new burdens on the Executive.

The lessons of history on the conduct of United States foreign affairs seem to show as more or less normal a kind of smoldering, occasionally open, warfare between the Executive and the

Legislature. There are periods of truce, periods of "cold war," periods of peace. But some degree of legislative-executive struggle, often "hot," has been a persistent characteristic of this nation. This condition, always annoying, becomes more and more preposterous in a world in which "power tensions" require a far more prompt national response than is possible under legislative-executive "guerrilla warfare" habits of mind and patterns of behavior.

Not only has this internecine warfare between the two major branches of the government responsible for the formation and control of foreign policy persisted. It has also become noticeably characteristic *within* each of those principal agencies, partly as a reflection of the deeper legislative-executive rift, partly from the nature of our representative system itself, which does not stress national unification of policy. Rather the system of elections samples the nature of sections and interests and settles for such unification as can be achieved through national pressure to limit narrower pressures.

THE ASSIGNMENT AND AIMS OF THE STUDY

Our original assignment was to seek out and define, so far as we could, those areas of the formation and control of foreign policy in which inquiry and study were particularly needed. It was at once evident that this task required first of all an assessment of the most important weaknesses in our present control of foreign affairs. This in turn led us back to larger and deeper topics. We were astonished to discover among ourselves a high degree of agreement on the nature of these critical problems, both in theory and in practice. As we came to specific recommendations, substantial divergences appeared; and yet we found, even here, a very considerable measure of consensus. Although our evidence and inquiry were necessarily restricted, we found this level of consensus highly significant for our first assignment, particularly as it turned up new emphases and approaches even to very old problems.

Many of the conclusions we reached have not been widely accepted. We are hardly equipped to pass judgment on our own views, but we do feel able to assert that *if* true, they are exceedingly important. We found them sufficiently persuasive to unite us at least in urging that our study does help to isolate some singularly important areas for further study, inquiry, and judgment.

So the body of this report deals with our argument on the major problems. The very substantial assertions and recommendations of this argument are in turn the underpinning of our recommendations as to the kinds of study that can most usefully be undertaken in the future.

The frame of reference established for this report is the conduct of United States foreign policy as a part of the "process" of American politics. But any analysis of process quickly reveals that the study of the instruments for the formation and control of foreign policy cannot be made by concentrating on the legislative and administrative structure alone, or even through the additional and relevant aspects of constitutional law, of historical precedents, and of the economic and political facets that make up the complex whole of American politics. What is needed to breathe life into the organic structure from which our foreign policy grows is an artistic, as much as a scientific, appreciation of the living evolution of actual foreign policies against the background of demands made upon American political leadership. Insights are more useful than statistics or formulae. These demands are made by the challenge of "power systems" as well as by "ideologies," and by the necessity of adjusting to the new United Nations organization for world relations. Our hope and aim is to unite a mature historical insight with valid perspectives in political science and administrative prudence in the analysis of our contemporary political "process."

The study of foreign policy as we see it would involve the assessment of the role of the President as well as of the Presidency, of men as well as of institutions. It could not deal with Congress merely in institutional terms without being mindful of the crucial impact on policy of such different individuals as Senator Vandenberg and Senator Taft. What we must perforce leave out of this study is the richer essence contributed by understanding deeply the protagonists, the personalities, that is, by the stuff of good biographies. That must be left to the labors of historical assessment. But we do not underestimate the wisdom of William Penn: "Governments are like clocks. As they are made by men, so may they be marred or ruined."

But even deprived of these deeper insights into personalities, our study has had the fascination of the most complicated type of analysis, in which the interplay of politics, economics, and military policy have to be examined within a framework of constitutional checks and balances—a federal system—and against the new and overwhelming external challenge to national survival by the world power situation.

How, too, can our brief report take adequate measure or really explain the acid corrosion of liberal values within the nation, resulting both from the crisis of our entire culture and from the real risks of externally organized plans for subversion, espionage, and psychological warfare from within?

At the same time it is clear that *substantive policies* themselves could not form the central core of a study of this scope. We do not aim at passing judgment on the moral validity or the strategic adequacy of particular foreign policies of the United States. We have, as far as we humanly could, avoided these temptations to play "Secretary of State" or "President." And this self-denial was not simply because in such an effort a wide divergence of views might result. Of course it is true, and useful, that more agreement is possible in analyzing the methods and processes of foreign policy formulation and control than in agreeing on all the complex substantive issues where the Latin tag is apt: *tot homines, tot sententiae.* But to study the *why* and *how* of policies does involve looking at the policies themselves. The incidental reference to substantive aspects of foreign policies comes from their "case" value, as they throw light upon the *nature of the process.* It is "process" —as reflected in political structure and administration—that concerns us.

Yet it must be admitted that the study of machinery and process is always aimed at improving the end product: There must be general assumptions about what constitutes a successful foreign policy and the criteria by which its adequacy, both as to its moral objectives and its survival value, can be assessed. This does not mean that we have insisted with each other (and we shall certainly not demand it from the reader) on agreement as to the details or even as to outlines of specific programs on contemporary foreign policy. It simply means that there must be consideration of the broad directional sweeps of that policy, its presuppositions—its ends and means. We came early to the realization that *assumptions underlie every approach to foreign policy making. The failure to make these explicit and critically valid seems to us a chief source of confusion and frustration.*

PRESUPPOSITIONS OF FOREIGN POLICY

The Philosophy of Human Nature Underlying United States Foreign Policy and Its Mechanisms

On one point there was complete agreement: Every sort of public policy depends for fruitful analysis on underlying assumptions about human nature. Method and means, too, depend on these, as well as ends. The rationale of United States foreign policy and of the public opinion which supports it have to be judged on these assumptions. Our eighteenth-century Founding Fathers had more than a modicum of distrust for unchecked power and for human frailty. The traditional nineteenth-century conception of American democracy clearly underestimated the element of "original sin" in human nature. On that view, "Progress" was thought to be the cure-all, achievable by liberal enlightenment, almost an inevitable by-product of democracy.

Yet, if "progressive" liberals in the nineteenth and into the twentieth century tended to adopt a "woolly" optimism based upon the disappearance of the evils of human nature through enlightened reason, operative in all men and applied by means of more and more democracy, they were no more "woolly" than Karl Marx's beatific salvation from economic necessity. This rationalized faith that the state was predestined to wither away merely through the socialization of private property was pure theology in Marx, with no vestige of real science. Indeed they were no more "woolly" than those conservatives who had an equally inexplicable optimism that big power groups would so balance each other and unleash general prosperity through private enterprise that a strong central government would hardly be needed, even to hold the ring. Conservatives in the twentieth century tended to change places with Thomas Jefferson in this matter in their emphasis on checking strong government (from regulating them) and relying on states' rights as an escape to less effective areas of control. But they were still in the old federalist tradition of holding on to the protection of the courts, until Franklin D. Roosevelt spoiled this refuge for them.

Deeply underlying the entire problem of the defects in American foreign policy is the possibility that recent times and the circumstances of national life have not bred a toughness of character and moral fiber; a tenacity in facing hard facts and an acquaintance with the ugly sides of human nature have not been, to an adequate degree, a part of the American heritage in recent generations. When the basic presuppositions of a nation's policy tend to neglect the existence of original sin, or of determinant evil, then that nation tends to neglect or avoid "power analysis," a fact which is in turn reflected in an absence of adequate preparedness in its defense establishment during times of peace. The sequel is a direct invitation to the evil-minded (who do not share our moral views or who ascribe them to hypocrisy) to capitalize on such military weakness and to make the most of it. In such an event, that the despoiler may come to ruin is small comfort to a world in agony.

We may have shown also a naïve faith in the ability of peoples to speak to peoples despite the intervention of their governments, or an equally short-sighted assumption that the United States could "go it alone." Indeed there appears to have been little in the cultural background of Americans generally that would have prepared them for an adequate estimate of the "brutalitarian" regimes.

Perhaps too deep a preoccupation with the economics of "peace and plenty" on the part of this nation has made it unwilling, and in that sense democratically unable, to face the "power element" in the world. Partly this has been a matter of the economic preoccupation being too deeply ingrained to throw off quickly when there has been necessity for facing a "power problem." A more realistic view of the evils of human nature as well as the potentials for good seems indicated if democracies are to survive in an age of unconventional warfare. The lesson is being learned, but at tragic cost—in some measure heavier cost because the effort involved in facing a ruthless system of imperialism has seemed too great for peacetime politics.

"ENDS" OF FOREIGN POLICY

Every study of the process and of the organization of the instruments for making and implementing foreign policy has as its ultimate end a good foreign policy or at least an adequate foreign policy. This poses the problem as to what criteria could be used for judging the success of a foreign policy. How shall we determine what are the best practical means and methods of forming policy without some criteria for judging its ends?

Of course this is not a search for formulae or for absolute answers. We must be content with the limits of the real world and with the probable rather than the ultimate. *We must start, at least, with the test of national survival.*

In a deep philosophical sense even so ultimate a disaster as the defeat of a nation and its temporary disappearance as an organic part of the world power system may not represent complete failure: defeated Greece, we are often assured, triumphed spiritually over Rome. The crucified Saviour transforms the life and hope of humanity in the Christian epic. Indeed, history is full of the spiritual paradox of the victor being subsequently overcome by the spirit of the vanquished. Yet it is not permitted to states to accept this type of historical judgment in terms other than their own survival. The first necessity of the state is the survival of its cultural life as a nation. Even if the "nation-concept" is to be transcended in the organization of the future, the transition must preserve the integrity of the parts in the merger. The best in Mazzini is his emphasis on this priority for a true cultural community in terms of modern political organization.

One could scarcely speak of a successful foreign policy for a Rome that had disappeared before the barbarian invasion, no matter what legacy may have been left to the West. On the other hand, the foreign policy of Constantinople proved to be relatively far more successful up to the middle of the 15th century, even though Byzantium had periods of almost utter corruption and spiritual disintegration. National survival is the first test for a successful foreign policy.

In one of our meetings Dr. Reinhold Niebuhr took up the difficult moral challenge of pacifism to this conclusion. We accepted as our own his position that, while Christian martyrdom as an ultimate and thoroughly consistent pacifism was a possible moral choice for an individual, pacifism could not be morally imposed upon a nation from within for two reasons: In the first place, since a nation is composed of the individuals in it, a part of the nation would be making the decision for all. Has even a majority the right to impose a death sentence to the survival of a minority's aspirations and national life—particularly if slavery may be involved? One can hardly conceive of an entire nation that would be willing to suffer collective martyrdom. On the record of our whole human past the will to group preservation is more universal than even the individual instinct for self-preservation. Most men will accept death for a cause. There is *some* faith for which they will die on the battlefield if they first have a chance to defend themselves. This is not martyrdom. They defend a cause with the hope to win. They would not accept the alternative offered by the enemy without a fight. Therefore it is not feasible to have one group that is martyr-minded decide an absolute pacifist destiny for the whole.

In the second place, in Dr. Niebuhr's analysis, a nation does not and can not have the religious concept of collective self-transcendence, whereas individuals may have a self-transcendent quality by which they face death with the certainty that their souls live on in immortality. Although a nation cannot be self-transcendent in the Niebuhrian sense, a nation that has a free constitutional system can adjust its own interests more readily within the context of a broader world interest than can a dictatorship.

Indeed, in a sense, nation versus world is just as false an antithesis as man versus state, even though in each case there is something to the antithesis. While the United Nations is not an end in itself, neither is the United States, because our present national values will survive only if we can maintain support for them outside, as well as inside, our borders. On the other hand, realistically considered, the United Nations may be able to survive only if the United States is powerful enough. This gives in a sense a distinct cast to foreign policy of *Machtpolitik* and of *raison d'état,* but with a difference: power is a means to a moral end—freedom for the world. Power, then, becomes an essential attribute of the state, and that power must be adequate at least to preserve intact the existing structure of the state and its existing territories. If a single state is incapable of this, it must combine with others, or utilize a balance of power to that end.

The very success of nineteenth-century liberalism and the particular setting of the United States, both in the geography and in the power complex of the time, tended to shield this country from the harsh realities which were commonplace necessities to the foreign policy of most other states. For us great standing armies were unnecessary, and even a navy of the first order was not essential under the power balance of the nineteenth century and our own isolationist aims.

This underestimation of the place of force and power as primary requisites of the state does not mark the earliest period of our national history. The origins of our constitutional system, in revolution from British rule and in the necessity for establishing internal order and foreign respect, produced a strong executive, and a concern for proper military strength. Fortunately for posterity the problem of military power was an intense preoccupation of the Founders of the Constitution during the early stages of our history when our involvement in European questions was still a matter affecting our own sur-

vival. The provisions of the Constitution of the United States
bear ample witness to this fact. In the Preamble, the "common
defense" precedes the "general welfare," as it does in the clause
granting Congress the power to raise taxes and to provide
funds. That may be accidental, but it was psychologically apt.
Six of the eighteen powers of Congress deal with war, more
or less directly, including of course the power to declare war.
This last was undoubtedly intended to prevent executive
usurpation of the control of national policy in this crucial area.
The powers of the President as Commander in Chief and the
provisions for military forces, including state militia, occupied
the most serious attention not only of the Constitutional Convention, but of the infant nation, confronting powerful European states with strong footholds on the North American continent (Britain, France, Spain, and later Russia).

But as these considerations receded the power setting
changed. The new setting furnished the "ecological" or the
"organic" factors which helped to set the pattern of American
foreign policy and to make natural the idea that mere extension
of law to the international regime could restrain the power
relationships which for other states were thought to be necessary realities of national struggles for survival.

However an even more important factor was the accompany-
ing moral tone and religious temper which gave rise to the
enthusiastic support of public opinion in the United States for
Hague Conferences, Bryan Treaties of Arbitration, Wilsonian
Fourteen Points, and the World Court—even if the League of
Nations itself fell victim to the Senate and to Wilson's own
stand on absolute principle. The less happy features of this
moralizing lay in the complete unrealism of outlawing war by
moral pronunciamentos without the backing of sanctions, as,
for example, in the Kellogg Pact.

The ghosts of Cobden and Bright may have dictated too
much of Mr. Cordell Hull's feeling than a greater degree of *t*

free trade and world-wide prosperity would obviate even the power struggles which Leninist-Stalinist imperialisms had spread from Moscow and the counter-revolutions which Fascism and Nazism had launched on the Continent. We Americans are familiar with Marxism as an economic fallacy. But we continue to overlook our own fallacy in sometimes giving primacy to the economic factor over the political, as is evidenced by our frequently expressed belief that merely by raising standards of living we can meet everywhere the fundamental challenge of communism. The acceptance of this pattern by Americans who would be horrified to be classed as "materialists" is highly ironical. The dogma of free trade became almost as magic a formula for achieving peace through "economism" as had the formula of Marxism through the dictatorship of the proletariat and the other fatalistic "economism" of capitalist downfall and inevitable transition into communism.

This habit of mind ("economism"), natural enough to a country whose nineteenth-century background was so free from real power struggles for survival, was also linked in the twentieth century to a great faith in moral ideas and principles as the better part of the "Shield of the Republic." Today there is a tendency to discount national-value concepts as part of the power equation. Yet who can doubt the impact of Woodrow Wilson's ideas not only on his own people but on the world, despite the fact that they were not given really lasting form in the League of Nations. Their full carry did not command the support of the United States itself in the struggle for the ratification of the Treaty of Versailles and the League of Nations. But this failure may well have been partly because the Treaty of Versailles so clearly looked to a power alignment buttressed by the Tripartite Defense Pact between France, England, and the United States, which we also rejected.

Any estimate of power in terms solely of physical force misses the lessons of history about the dynamics of faith and the bearing of moral purpose on morale. It is part of the pseudo-scientific spirit which tends to discount things spiritual and intangible.

The current reaction against morals in politics is probably due in great part to the confusion of *morals* with *moralizing* during the twenties and well into the thirties. To have coupled naval disarmament with nothing stronger than the Kellogg Pact or even reliance upon the World Court was a policy totally lacking in realism, the substitution of an "escapist" moral homily for active support and will to perform. The test of true morals is to believe in them strongly enough to translate them into facts by acts. The Nine-Power Treaty for the Pacific was in itself not unrealistic. But the whole complex of settlements for the Pacific reached in Washington in 1922 was not joined to an adequate emphasis upon the security also of the Atlantic world. This total security, furthermore, could hardly have been guaranteed, as many Americans believed, by mere adherence to the World Court and reliance upon a regime of international law without willingness to back that by sanctions and to insist upon the necessary machinery for its enforcement. The nadir of our foreign policy was seen in the neutrality acts of the thirties, stemming from the investigations of the Nye Committee into the armament manufacturers ("Merchants of Death"). The childishness of the assumption that we could stop war by controlling the private manufacture of arms and eliminating trade with belligerents was the extreme position. Even the less extreme assumption that neutrality, strictly pursued by the United States, could keep us out of world wars in the future and insulate us from the power struggle manifestly brewing for the control of Europe and Asia was equally illusory.

The spiritual values and myths of America determined its

total policy through a combination of moral idealism, magic formulae, and the behavior of a power system natural to its setting and to its historic evolution. Its foreign policy therefore emphasized survival far less than did the foreign policies of other states until well along into the middle of the twentieth century. It has been argued that a more prescient foreign policy on the part of a growing colossus like the United States might have prevented both world wars by building up military strength and throwing its weight into the power balance. But such an argument probably assumes a type of leadership and a degree of wisdom in public response that is completely out of historical perspective. It is impossible to demand of any nation's foreign policy a response and behavior on the part of that nation which is wise with the wisdom of "after the event." The terrifying query is always present in human affairs as to whether a nation can learn the most painful lesson of the price of survival from any other master than necessity and the punishment of disaster.

IS NATIONAL MORALITY POSSIBLE IN A WORLD OF POWER POLITICS?

During our year of study we continually reverted to discussion of the place of morality in a world in which power politics is such an evident factor. A measure of agreement emerged in tentative answers to the following questions, which amounted to recurrent themes in our discussions:

If survival is the ultimate test of a state, what escape is there from power politics based frankly on the necessity of force and the organization of foreign policy with this primary emphasis? Does this more "realistic" view of foreign policy demand putting aside morality except as pretext and the adoption of Machiavellian estimates of diplomacy by a type of democratic leadership operating also by the "Big Lie," although admittedly the Lie would have to be more subtle than it need be in a dictatorship?

Our consensus on this syndrome of questions was that the old "moralizing" analyses of foreign policy have tended to provoke extreme reactions in the direction of defining politics only in terms of physical factors, emphasizing military force. This is a healthy reaction in so far as it is recognition that states as such cannot survive without a sound power base against a present crusading threat of world domination from Moscow, as from the Axis powers in the preceding decade. But when it proceeds to the conclusion that real power is not based also on a deep sense of moral conviction—faith in a mission— it is mistaken. These latter values are not physical factors. Yet they govern the responses of human beings and supply the whole dynamics which make any system weak or strong. *Democracies must therefore combine morality with power.* Indeed it is their inevitable nature to have to make up for their lack of emphasis on force and their tardy preparation for defense by extra reserves of spiritual energy which can be tapped in crisis.

WOODROW WILSON: POWER AND MORALITY UNDER INTERNATIONAL ORGANIZATION

The attacks currently being made on efforts like those of President Wilson to introduce moral principles into the conduct of foreign policy and to embody them in international agreements, formulating them into law with enforceable sanctions, sails today under the banner of "realism." It is difficult to distinguish from *Realpolitik.* Its present vogue stems from a reaction against our previous reliance upon moralizing, as we have suggested, rather than on a firm line of principle, such as the protection of weaker states from aggression through united

force, even where no immediate national survival or even narrow concept of national interest is involved. The attack on Wilson's policies neglects the fact that he was not unaware of the
nature of force in combining morality with the necessary power
to achieve its objectives. What he wanted was *sufficient* force to
stabilize, rather than just enough to offer a precarious balance,
always in danger of upset. A balance of power, which is the
"realistic" remedy now proposed, is well enough as a proximate
objective if the force representing freedom and resistance to
imperialistic aggression is the weaker side and requires to
be built up to a balance for sheer survival. That may well be
the present case. But a balance of power alone that does not
aim at imposing restraints on future aggression of every order
by establishing an over-balance to support a world system of
law is surely not a solution. Indeed this so-called realism looks
uncommonly like surrendering to the devil all the best tricks.

Put it this way: The concept of a national interest which is
limited to the protection only of those lines of action that
promote the immediate satisfaction of a nation's economic
requirements and the resultant political aims for protecting
this type of national objective has very little chance of aligning,
on a stable basis, sufficient power behind it to meet the challenge of powerful aggression bent on changing the world, such
as comes from crusading communism. Moscow would be left
with all the promises, and the strength built on these false
promises, to unite the world and to supply its own brand of
"liberation" from the capitalists. It is not enough for us to show
that this liberation enslaves and attempts to suppress really
free science as well as rational change. Any balance of power
based on national interests alone also lacks the dynamic of a
promise of either a secure or of a really free world. It can
maintain security only on the tenuous basis of continuous
"arrangements," without a real foundation in commitments to
common policy among the members who comprise the free-

world part of the United Nations. We have to oppose a faith that is coerced to a pattern of world order by our faith that is free to take world order only in the degree that "order" is compatible with change and free development.

This is far from meaning that morality should substitute ineffectual performance or abstract ideals for the power systems necessary to its effective operation in international relations. Every statesman has first of all to think of survival. But he is no statesman unless he sees that survival can be more readily assured, both in the short and long runs, by uniting the policies of those with similar systems and beliefs who also wish to assure survival. The dignity of human personality and the freedom from totalitarian subversion and coercion afford such a common line of interest, just because they are also the precondition of freedom and real moral community. National self-determination for satellite countries now works for our side.

If democracies are seduced into giving up their essential strength as proponents of freedom and the conditions which assure the development of human morality in the world at large, they have suffered a major and perhaps a catastrophic defeat in the battle of ideas.

On the other hand, to push democratic dogma into demanding self-determination for peoples who are completely unready for it is to neglect the lesson of "trusteeship" which Wilson incorporated into the structure of the League of Nations. The free world must require credentials for the assumption of national self-determination and must protect the use of natural resources for world purposes (as well as the rights of natives) without conceding a legal fiction of sovereignty to tribes only slightly removed from savagery. Partnership can be real only among peoples who are something like equal in capacity for self-government. This, too, Wilson clearly foresaw.

In short, it is not enough to rely on pure power balance and on narrow conceptions of national interest. If we hope to prevent aggression through pooled power, we must search for and support by word and deed a common ground for international purpose among the free nations. Otherwise we sacrifice not only principles but the future of whole peoples. This would be to give up—along with our heritage of moral leadership—the best method of guaranteeing our chances of national survival. No nation which loses its inner faith and its sense of mission can rally others, even for a precarious balance of power.

We must admit that this leaves the problem of democratic leadership always face to face with the necessity for achieving the difficult combination of high moral principles and realistic, shrewd diplomacy along with the maintenance of domestic political survival in an atmosphere of internal pressures and counterpulls. In short, the democratic leader must work within party mechanisms. He must protect the basic values of the system, which include the moral ultimacy of the individual personality, and yet protect national security, which at times may deny the moral ultimacy of specific groups of individuals, such as eighteen-year old males (unconsulted as to votes) who are necessary to defend the nation at a given moment. He must persuade his people to sometimes painful sacrifices and decisions that depend upon foresight and yet retain and abide by their suffrage at the polls. He must, as a political leader, elicit from his people the positive support of their organized politics as well as their better natures. At the same time, in the conduct of foreign policy, he must prove himself as "wise as the serpent" and yet not allow other nations to think of him as "harmless as the dove"—except in the purity of his motives.

DEMOCRACY AND SURVIVAL

Another recurrent theme with which we were concerned also related morals to the facts of power and of human nature, but it turned specifically on *the intensity of the issue of national survival in our times.* The question was raised in all sincerity and seriousness as to whether the increasingly secret nature of the most important decisions that underlie our foreign policy do not undermine the possibility of democratic control, rooted in informed opinion. The MacArthur hearings, like the controversy over the B-36 bomber vis-à-vis the giant naval aircraft carrier, may seem to have left very little of our high strategy to tell Moscow or for that matter to inform our own public and that of our Allies.* But the real issues on which all basic policy rests may be crucially conditioned by secrets never really opened up: for example, on the relative production of atomic weapons; the efficacy of bacteriological weapons; the value of surprise in new types of warfare; possible new devices opened to submarine warfare; vulnerability of harbors and sea lanes to new types of mines; and progress in the making of guided missiles and contact fuses. These secret devices may render obsolete, or at least far less effective, whole armaments of conventional weapons and whole strategic and tactical plans based on conventional estimates of strength. In brief, how can either Congress or the electorate, to which both President and Congress are responsible, really understand the issues which condition modern strategy such as the role of guided missiles, new uses of mines and submarines, biological warfare, and the full implications of A- and H-bombs? Stark tragedy may lie at the end of miscalculations in the nightmare world into which science has led us. Is democracy with its open procedures and its "open covenants openly arrived at" better able to survive than a system which can strike without warning and which can organize strategy without regard for the pressures of internal opinions, or the delays and "blocks" involved in

---

* What little secrecy was left on this point was stripped in late June (1951) by "leaks" from the Senate Committee of the Armed Services, which revealed the exact number and state of repair of this major weapon for atomic retaliation (the B-36).

democratic procedures? All this is added to the natural drift toward Caesarism in complex and highly organized societies where the possibility of effective administrative mechanisms tends to outgrow that of democratic control in any case.

We reached no real consensus on the forecast which this new ordeal for democracy has presented. The question might well have to be left an open one. Hopeful signs were discerned in the degree to which the public has so far responded to strong democratic leadership and has willingly borne the burdens imposed in confronting threats to survival. It was argued, convincingly, that the freest nations have been those that had the most complex development, and that this had not led to Caesarism in the major contemporary instances. Technical power, too, has rested on the side of freedom.

However, we recognized ugly signs also present, for example: fear might produce a continuing threat to civil liberties; the kinds of decisions really basic to the policies evolved by the Joint Chiefs of Staff and the National Security Council could hardly be evaluated in any adequate way by mass opinion, by the views of the "common man," even when filtered through all the organizational system of a mature democracy. The role of the responsible general executive clearly is to be the reasonable medium between the professional specialist and the untutored reactions of public opinion and even the pressure-ridden legislature. In sum, it was concluded that democracy might adjust responsibility to provide a balance between discretion for the executive, professional military and political estimates, and common sense control by Congress and by public opinion as to basic direction.

"ONE-WORLDISM"

Another general problem which ran through our discussions was rooted in the coercive kind of logic that lies behind the attraction of the "One World Now" idea. If the import of the preceding question may be called "the threat of militaristic Caesarism" to democratically controlled foreign policy, buttressed by the necessity for greater and greater secrecy, the third theme may be called the "solution by world federalism." In a sense these two alternatives are often treated as if they were the horns of a dilemma. To the world federalists, the alternatives are sometimes reduced even more simply to "perish or unite." Has this coercive demand to "unite," as the sole guarantee of morality, in itself some elements of the greatest danger to democracy and to genuine morality? How can we achieve "One World Now" without a preventive war to suppress Moscow, or without accepting the form of world government which would mean the inevitable triumph of the nuclear "closed" system of Moscow as against the disorganized "open" systems of the free world?

It was clear from our discussions that short of this absolute "solution" through one world government (agreed to be both utopian and dangerous) the realistic basis of international relations lies in multilateral methods. These impose entirely new conditions upon the conduct of foreign policy in any one state. Fundamental to this approach is recognition and working acceptance of the fact that domestic politics are so completely intermingled with the problems of foreign policy that no nation is an "island unto itself." Even more, its fate depends upon the strength and help of many other nations, given the unlikely possibility that a nation could so organize its own power system as to escape external dependence. The President of the United States has, then, to address himself to a world audience for support, while at the same time his political fate rests in the hands of an American electorate.

Either alternative (isolation or leadership in the free United Nations) imposes a heavy load upon a world power like the

United States, which far outstrips other nations in economic resources and potential for military organization. To build up the strength of other free nations leads to accepting limits upon our own freedom of action if we choose to work within the framework of a United Nations. United or not, the members tend to think differently about the business of their survival as parts of the whole. Europe, for example, is afraid of our involvement in the Far East and demands a check on our policy. A heavy, perhaps a continuing, burden of foreign economic and military aid may be imposed on us as a minimum condition for free world organization. But to "go it alone" would require control of vital overseas resources of strategic materials and bases. This would necessitate a type of imperialism antithetical to the American mind, as well as a continuing military organization on a scale hardly likely to be permanently compatible with democratic procedures and constitutional protections.

We faced these real difficulties without conceding them to be dilemmas. But we are agreed that the mere existence of international organization is not in itself a guarantee of the absolute moral rightness of decisions taken in its name. Immanuel Kant, in his essay *Zum ewigen Frieden,** probably correctly concluded that the moral basis for world law could only be found if the component states were what he called in eighteenth-century terms "republican"—in modern terms "constitutional." The United Nations contains many states which are certainly far short of this position. Few of its members represent real constitutional maturity, and the hard core of the Soviet block would destroy constitutional systems everywhere, were it able to do so.

To the degree that democracies have to fight continuously for survival, they tend toward authoritarian forms to oppose

---

* *Toward a Perpetual Peace* is the usual title in English translation. See also C. J. Friedrich, *Inevitable Peace*.

modern totalitarianism. It is at once a condition of healthy democratic development in the world to establish an international regime of law capable of assuring peace; and, conversely, a precondition for the establishment of such an international regime that it rest on constitutional democracies. The world community has not evolved to a point where either Britain or the United States would agree that the nation's fate should rest upon any form of world organization wherein totalitarian systems like those of Russia or China were given weight according to population. And even if India aims at democracy, could it be seriously weighted in a world order on the basis of "one man, one vote"? In short, even if constitutional forms were followed in a world state, there would be the greatest reluctance to concede central powers over our entire economic as well as our entire political life to a federal world government. In hard facts, this probably means we cannot stake our national existence upon the decisions of the United Nations should they ever go contrary to our own views on the matter of national survival. We do not need to rely on our veto in the United Nations, as Russia does, because we do not aim at secrecy and conquest and power moves *against* others. We do not have to protect a closed system from all outside inspection or to hold our own view to be fatally right. But we might under some conditions have to act for survival even without United Nations support.

Yet this does not absolve a democracy from attempting to find a basis for moral agreement, for full utilization of the will to freedom and national self-determination, and for the protection of human rights common to all free systems. It simply means a more strenuous effort to organize the free world and to accept the necessary sacrifices and burdens of an adequate foreign policy to that end. It does not mean, on the other hand, the substitution of an illusory guarantee through "formula" for real moral and military power based on our own efforts.

DEMOCRATIC LEADERSHIP

A fourth recurrent theme was found in the role of democratic leadership in the struggle for democratic survival. The complexity of the crisis, as well as its urgency, makes the necessity for wise democratic leadership all the greater. Yet democracy, in its traditional theory, has tended to evade or ignore the problem of leadership. Having originated in the affirmation of the natural rights of men against the divine right of kings, democracy has tended to regard the theory of leadership (if not the fact) with suspicion, lest recognition of the decisive need for leadership be a back door through which new divine rights might enter. There is nothing inherently anti-democratic in the sociology of governing groups; yet the most searching analysts of leadership (Michels) and of ruling elites (Mosca, Pareto) have had their preponderant influence in anti-democratic circles. Against the leadership doctrine, democratic theory has tended to trail off into vague or sentimental assertions that the leader becomes important merely as the representative of the people.

While it is certainly true that the democratic leader must represent the people, he is bound to be a good deal more than just a rubber-stamp for their preferences and policies. If only because, in the contemporary world, policies are far too complicated to be definable in terms which can be settled by referendum, a considerable measure of executive discretion is inescapable. Even in simpler days, the democratic leader made personal and creative contributions of high importance to national policies. The real distinction between democratic and authoritarian societies lies, not in the existence of leaders or elites, but in the ways in which they are chosen, exercise power, and are held accountable.

The democratic leader has exerted his leadership neither through the divine right of the monarchs he displaced nor through the ruthless charism of the totalitarian leaders who rose to challenge him. Where the one ignores the great mass of the people and the other seeks to violate and debauch the mass, turning it into the mob, the democratic leader at his best has treated the people as rational and responsible individuals, seeking while he submits his views to them to educate them intellectually to the complexity of problems and to educate them morally to the necessity for decision. The democratic leader is thus no rubber stamp; his responsibility is to provide initiative. But his initiative is only that available to any democratic citizen; it seeks to develop the moral and rational, not the sheepish or swinish, faculties in the people; and it succeeds, not because it produces an orgasm in the mass, but because it breaks the mass down into reasonable individuals, not drily ratiocinative, but full men, in whom morality, emotion, and reason are inseparably intertwined.

Such leadership, obviously, is difficult to find, difficult to sustain. It requires a society which produces such men, fosters them, rewards them; it requires a political environment through which they may rise; it requires political mechanisms which neither impede their ability to exercise initiative nor their will to exercise it within the limits of morality and rationality.

To summarize, democratic foreign policy faces more problems than do other systems because a democracy must insist upon a moral basis for the organization of its own system (Bill of Rights, constitutional procedures) and in addition the maintenance of a moral order in international relations. However, a particular moral system may require a kind of economic structure such as that involved in the concept of a "welfare state," on which the financial and resource necessities of national security may heavily impinge. All this puts to those who are concerned with democracy and its possible control of foreign policy some peculiarly difficult questions. They are questions of the interrelationship of desirable *moral* ends with the necessary ends as well as means of power, and with the realistic workings of human nature. These interrelationships are implicit and run through all problems connected with foreign policy. Yet it was interesting and perhaps significant how readily we reached general concurrence on the nature of the moral ends to be sought.

Foreign policy, on this reading, is not to be construed simply in terms of morals, or of economics, or of purely military power, or even of cultural determinism. *The conduct of foreign policy represents at its most dramatic point the struggle of a nation's "spirit" with its "fate."* Tragedy is always possible—for not all challenges either *can* be met or *will* be met. The coercion of force and the competition of power systems are always present. In practice this has branded the professionals of diplomacy with a marked cast of Machiavellianism. To study foreign policy is to attempt to find simple solutions among what often appear to be hopeless complexities. Yet this is only one of the riddles of the Sphinx which is continuously presented to the human race. Its urgency in our times forces it the more sharply on our attention.

The adequacy of a democratic foreign policy therefore demands at a minimum the following criteria: survival, constitutionalism, democratic morality, economic and military sufficiency, and the achievement of a context of international organization suitable to establish at least a reasonable degree of stability in international relations.

"MEANS" IN FOREIGN POLICY—MATRIX OF THE INQUIRY

Ends in foreign policy, however, take on their meaning in the real world of historical force in terms of the means chosen to realize them. Means, for purposes of our study, primarily relate to institutions, political, economic, and cultural. The framework of a government for the formation of policy and its methods of action in this sense constitute the means about which our discussion has principally revolved. Four general themes seem to us to be the focal points about which contemporary difficulties in the formulation and conduct of American foreign policy could be grouped:

The choice, first, of institutional mechanisms is related to the separation of powers. We have centered our attention specifically on executive-legislative relations. While the nature of the courts in the American system and their part in the shaping of constitutional law are highly relevant, their place requires more extensive study than is permitted by the scope of this report. Suffice it here to point out that fortunately the constitutional law laid down by the Supreme Court has not in itself tended too greatly to handicap whatever strengthening of the executive powers is possible without a radical change in our constitutional framework. The discussion which follows attempts to lay out the major problems arising from the basic separation of powers and to ask questions which we propose to formulate as the basis of our own inquiry and for subsequent study, recommended for follow-up by others.

The second theme is the relation of public spirit (not just "opinion") and the electoral process to the ultimate control of foreign policy in a democracy. The development of this point carries the study of political parties and of pressure groups and the roles of leaders and professionals a stage further and raises once more what we judge to be the most significant questions.

A third study of means in relation to ends considers some of the problems and mechanisms relating to national security in the balance of its protection with individual freedom. Procedures for protecting the individual and their possible conflicts with national security are brought in at this point with suggestions for resolution. We feel, too, that the military-civilian balance is a basic study of means for uniting power and principle.

Finally, we thought it necessary to consider the methods by which the conduct of foreign policy has been broadened by United States membership in the United Nations. Here, too, questions of organization and new balances reflect themselves in techniques that are just beginning to show their impact on our diplomatic mechanisms and on our political process.

We hope by this framework to show the way in which problems of foreign policy are inextricably connected with a basic philosophy of politics and with an interpretation of the working of men and mechanisms in institutional expressions. It seemed to us that by framing questions in areas where research and interpretation seem weakest, we could make the most useful contribution. Their value lies in suggesting that most studies of policy have been deficient in not examining, systematically, the assumptions on which their conclusions inevitably rest. This consensus represents a genuine result, a precipitate, if one may use a physical term, of our whole Study.

The following questions are presented more or less in outline as a framework for the more detailed discussion in the next section. They are stated more as questions than as propositions. Answers will necessarily relate to our conclusions on the ends of foreign policy. But for purposes of convenient analysis, we have attempted to separate general problems from specific mechanisms, admitting by this that institutions alone do not define our problems. Institutions must be related to the broader inquiries into human nature, force and power, leadership and opinion—that we have treated under the realm of ends. We have chosen to frame these questions on means in order to focus the basic issues that arise from our constitutional pattern and our politics:

THE CONSTITUTIONAL PATTERN IN THE FORMULATION AND
CONTROL OF FOREIGN POLICY

The Separation of Powers

Can the American version of "separation of powers" (specifically, our present form of executive-legislative relationships) afford a unified and continuous support for the type of foreign policy necessary to meet the conditions of international reciprocity and of national survival? What method of electing the Executive and the Legislature will do most to lead the American people to unite in support of foreign policy?

The Executive

What new devices are essential within the Executive Branch to increase the adequacy of formulation, control, and implementation in the crucial new role of foreign policy as the matrix of all policy? What will be the effect of such new devices on the Cabinet, on executive departments and staffs, on relations to Congress and party organization?

The Legislature

Can a legislature elected so largely in response to state and local attitudes toward national issues, with seniority as a determining basis for its committee leadership, and with little party discipline, meet the challenge for constructive participation in the conduct of foreign policy? What can be expected of the contributions of legislative staffs, of committee reorganization, of increased responsible control through party leadership (policy committees, etc.) and of better organization of Congress for consultation with the Executive in the formative stages of policy? What are the effects of the special positions of the Rules, Appropriations, and Executive Expenditures Committees in both Houses? Can special and "select" committees in both Houses be constructively used to broaden congressional information and support? Joint committees?

The Ultimate Control in a Democracy—Public Opinion and the Electoral Process

Are sources of information adequate for wise public judgment on the real merits of complex issues in foreign policy? What is the role of official information services in this process and, in particular, the information operations of the Department of State? With the means, public and private, at its disposal, is there any reason to believe that public opinion in a democracy possesses the innate capacity to judge adequately the merits of the substantive issues in foreign policy? How is this related to the electoral process for assuring responsibility to opinion?

The Political Party as an Integrating Factor and Conduct of United States Foreign Policy

If foreign policy calls for toughness and shrewdness as well as for moral purpose, how can healthy democratic politics produce leaders sufficient to meet the challenge of the times? Must a democratic leader "fool the people?" What type of elective machinery and selective processes within it will achieve effective political leadership, and an administrative class suitable for diplomacy and foreign service? What will be the relations of such leaders and such a professional group to public support and criticism? How can responsibility and control be organized at political and administrative levels?

POWER, PRINCIPLE, AND POLICY: MECHANISMS AND METHODS

NATIONAL SECURITY AND INDIVIDUAL FREEDOM

What kind of framework of opinion and attitudes is needed to support an insistence on basic liberties, and does a prolonged crisis impose intolerable strain on this framework? What is the proper role of the courts in the protection of civil liberties in relation to a foreign policy whose central objective is national security? What security policies, immigration controls, and state organizations of secret policy and intelligence are involved in an adequate modern foreign policy? What bearing have court decisions, legislative acts, and executive policies on these facets of the problem?

THE MILITARY-CIVILIAN BALANCE

What is the proper connection between the military and the civilian factors in the modern democracy of the United States? What is the basic relationship between power and policy? What institutional arrangements are necessary both in the Executive and in Congress? What special safeguards and checks do modern circumstances impose (a) in military adequacy, and (b) in civilian control of ultimate policy and power?

UNITED STATES MEMBERSHIP IN THE UNITED NATIONS: MULTILATERAL DIPLOMACY AND THE TECHNIQUES OF ALLIANCE

The United States government, though clear in its basic responsibility for the survival of its own society, is closely and necessarily involved in connection with larger groupings of varying size and strength. A specific and important aspect of this connection is the increased use of "multilateral diplomacy," both in the United Nations and in the multiplicity of organizations surrounding the North Atlantic Community. Is this activity merely a new outlet for the pursuit of the "national interest," or is it the beginning of a new and higher interest and obligation? Does it impose special requirements upon the makers of foreign policy, and if so, what are they?

These questions suggest a connecting thread which runs

through the discussions of both "ends" and "means." They continually pose the alternative of more executive discretion within democratic machinery as against the alternative of more direct and detailed control of foreign policy by Congress.

Differences of emphasis as to which of these alternatives is more important are not simply matters of temperament. The historic swing of the pendulum as between the growth of executive and congressional power suggests that the compulsion of necessity for effective foreign policy in times of crisis has always increased the discretionary powers of the President. Since, however, we appear to live in almost perpetual crisis, any examination of the "process of politics" which is focused on foreign policy must attempt to find a combination of popular control and responsibility with the necessary increase in executive discretion.

Is this a true dilemma? Our discussions showed that military thinking is characterized by the necessity of eliminating dilemmas in order to have a firm plan for every contingency. But plans for all contingencies are not available in the processes of democracy. The very nature of democracy is to permit changes in plans, and to insist on continuous revisions of policy where circumstances change and political support varies. This is a hard doctrine, and it bears almost as heavily on the professionals of diplomacy as on the military professionals. The former are accustomed to dealing with ever-shifting balances of foreign combinations of power and changed objectives. To be exposed to an adjustment in internal changes seems to the foreign office of every democratic country an intolerable burden. Yet it is a load that must be borne. The problem which the following sections analyze is how best to adjust the load to the possibilities of our inherited institutions with whatever help we may pray for through an increased wisdom of leadership and in more understanding popular support.

SUMMARY

A summary view of the ground which we have laid out in this introduction may be alarming in its scope. Even with the elimination of many important problems, those on which we have centered attention raise questions of such ultimate character that one may despair of finding answers. We do not, indeed, profess to have done more than to indicate the lines along which answers may be fruitfully sought. Our emphasis from the beginning has been to look at the assumptions on which foreign policy must be based, to study the criteria with which to judge its ends and aims, and to relate the whole to the mechanisms by which foreign policy is formulated and put into effect.

There is a further broad range of research in what may be termed the philosophy of history (sometimes treated under sociology), which attempts to find scientific patterns and formulae for this sort of inquiry. We have indicated our own assumptions—but not with the hope of producing formulae, least of all magic formulae. The analyses of the particular problems selected for treatment that follow have in a general way one primary value. If our selection and emphasis and the conclusions that we have reached *as to what is important* seem reasonably valid, they do suggest a broad reorientation in the types of studies of the working of American institutions made by historians, political scientists, and others. They particularly suggest that, difficult as the task may be, only the highest level of mature historical insight, coupled with a willingness to face with some boldness the new factors in world politics can offer any hope of transcending the routine which so usually marks descriptive political studies. Without tracing conclusions back to their fundamental assumptions and testing those assumptions against our best insights into the nature of human nature and its application to foreign policy, research may be a very wasteful product, misleading in its pretense to "scientific method."

We have stressed the presuppositions, the ends that shape the means in a democratic foreign policy. But ideas, as even Hegel said, must take on "hands and feet," that is, our means also limit and in some ways determine ends. They take on form in the means of improving the formulation and conduct of United States foreign policy. No grand design is better than the capacity of the instrument which carries it out. We propose to select crucial points for study, emphasizing neglected approaches and significant alternatives. Our object and hope is to stimulate further and deeper insights into these problems. We have selected them because they seemed to be at once the most lacking and the most needed elements in the approach of American students to the processes of foreign policy making.

PART ONE

THE EFFECT OF THE AMERICAN
CONSTITUTIONAL AND FEDERAL
ORGANIZATIONAL PATTERN
ON THE FORMULATION AND CONDUCT
OF FOREIGN POLICY

HISTORICALLY our constitutional system took its whole character from the Founding Fathers' views on combining with the necessary "common defense" for purposes of survival a "firm and perpetual union" that would also assure to the American people the "blessings of liberty" and the "general welfare." But the views of eighteenth-century Americans on human nature left the assurance of these ends dependent upon special institutional organization of power and responsibility. To balance fear of too great power of the central government (of men, not of laws) three things were incorporated into the Constitution: (1) an emphasis upon strong state governments and powers reserved to the people (including the necessary concurrence of two thirds of the Senate on treaty commitments); (2) a system of checks and balances that included the separation and sharing of powers, judicial review, *plus* a strong Executive; and (3) a federal union which, with the support of extraordinary majorities, could cement the entire nation and provide adequately for its common defense.

The subsequent history of the growth of nationalism in the United States has shown an inevitable alteration of these original balances. Through the development of a national party system, democratic responsibility to a national electorate has grown to what amounts almost to the direct election of the President, as well as the direct election of Senators. The federal union has tended to become more and more a national system with "escape" devices in foreign policy to evade the two-thirds requirement for Senate ratification of treaties. While checks and balances remain, along with certain vestiges of federalism, such as two Senators for every state regardless of population, the compulsions of foreign policy, even more than those of domestic policy, have made us aware of the dangerous contradictions in our present political order.

II

THE SEPARATION OF
POWERS

HE CONSTITUTION did not define with precision the respective roles of the Congress and of the President in foreign policy. By giving the House, the Senate, and the President independent tenure and different terms of office, the Constitution set up a system which, along with the distinctive powers of our federal judiciary, we call the separation of powers. But in other ways our Constitution blurred the boundaries between the powers. This system of checks and balances, which includes sharing powers as well as separating them, produces a sort of marriage relationship which falls under what some psychologists would call the "antagonistic-cooperation" variety.

The House and Senate are nearly equal in power. But the President is the acknowledged political leader of the nation, so legislative leadership cannot be organized in either House of Congress, but must come from the Executive. On the other hand, the Executive must depend on the laws and on the appropriations of Congress for the organization and support of the departments. If congressional committees choose to use this dependence to control minute details of administration, it is almost impossible to prevent them from so doing—short of applying the full weight of party control in the legislature. This remedy is too drastic to be used often, and it is often lacking in the loose organization of legislative party control.

The resulting ambiguity has caused a continuing dispute throughout American history regarding the amount of authority and discretion that Congress should grant to the Executive. Congress can hardly take over and direct foreign policy itself, except piecemeal through its committees. But it can and does refuse to let the Executive Branch have enough power or means to do so in a steady, coordinated manner. It alternates between the techniques of "guerrilla warfare" and of "cold war." The emphasis is normally on some kind of warlike technique between the two branches—except in time of war. Then the Legislature tends to devolve too much power on the Executive and to resign its critical functions in foreign policy. After war, Congress normally tends to express its dammed-up criticism in a series of sporadic explosions. The Chief Executive, apart from his normal prestige as party leader and ability to mobilize public opinion, can appeal to the people directly, over the head of Congress—but only through a general election every four years. The party mechanism and the mid-term elections do not pose national issues to the electorate at other times.

When there has been no widespread sense of urgency in foreign affairs, or when the Executive has had no clear ideas about foreign policy, congressional committees and Congress as a whole have tended to keep close control of such matters as can be brought within their province. When national security has been uppermost in people's minds and when quick decisions have been required for its protection, the President, with the support of the Congress, has assumed a much stronger role. But the regular tendency has been for strong leadership to be dissipated with the passing of a crisis, and for the detailed checks of congressional committees (sometimes at variance with each other as well as with the Executive) to make impossible the maintenance of a coordinated and disciplined policy.

Braking or supplanting the initiative of the President is probably the general pattern of congressional attitude on foreign policy during "normal times." Particularly in the crucial period of the thirties it was a serious handicap to the conduct of American foreign policy that the President was not permitted to be the responsible initiator, even if not the sole director, of foreign policy. The Constitution certainly intended him to be the former, at least. It was a handicap, too, that the Cabinet was not a closely knit council of political advisers, that the Secretary of State was often not supported by his Cabinet colleagues in foreign affairs, that the military services were poorly integrated with each other and with the rest of the Executive Branch, and that the traditional facilities for reconciling legislative and executive interests in the conduct of foreign policy were no longer adequate, if indeed they ever had been.

British and Dominion democracies seem less plagued with such interior organizational hazards to the smooth conduct of foreign policy. But continental democracies fare as ill or worse. Compare, for example, the way in which the Marshall Plan was handled by the British, French, and American varieties of democratic government:

THE ENACTMENT OF THE ECONOMIC COOPERATION ADMINISTRATION LAW IN 1948 AS AN EXAMPLE

Although the Lend Lease Legislation of World War II marks the real beginning of Congress's new role in foreign policy, owing to the new relationship of foreign policy to financial appropriations for foreign aid, the Economic Cooperation Administration legislation is a more useful and dramatic example. Wartime does not furnish a normal model.

During the formative period of the legislative history of

the Marshall proposals nothing was more striking than the elaborate complications of three different exploratory committees appointed by the President—the Krug Committee, the Harriman Committee, and the Council of Economic Advisers—as well as the legislative counter-check, the Herter Select Committee on Foreign Aid—all analyzing the problem, sometimes in conflicting terms. On the other hand, the British representatives who headed the Organization for European Economic Cooperation team, a mere handful, had a completely worked-out program and a well-marked line of national policy from the earliest stages. By dint of having a unified policy of their own, they secured some unity even among their continental partners in prospective benefactions.

Moreover, the British parliamentary discussions, in contrast to American legislative debates, were marked by a remarkable range of agreement. Apart from a narrow band of fellow travelers on the left and an even narrower band of Tory "little imperialists" on the right, British parliamentary opinion found little quarrel with the program. This was not just the consensus of desperation. The furor within continental governments (for example, France) on the same issue—stirred up of course by communists—shows that division was possible even in war-spent democracies, badly needing aid to survive.

The British Treasury, through the Board of Trade and the Foreign Office, as usual played a dominant role in the making of requirements estimates. Other British departments had had their say at the levels of the Cabinet Secretariat and the Cabinet itself. Above all, there was no such unseemly spectacle (from the point of view of the truly professional requirement of unifying a foreign policy) as occurred in the battles between the authorizing committees in each house of the American Congress (Foreign Affairs and Foreign Relations) and again in the Appropriations Committees, which succeeded in attacking already enacted legislative policy by making substantial alterations in the authorized amounts and inserting new legislative provisions in the Act.

In the United States the pulling and hauling of private interests over legislation, representing as they did agriculture, coal, shipping, maritime labor, machine tools and the like, marked the whole congressional struggle over the nature and content of the Economic Cooperation Administration bill.

Even within the executive departments, the Bureau of the Budget and the State Department were known to be at such loggerheads as to organizational patterns that Congress finally wrote in its own ideas of organization. It did so only after calling in (at Senator Vandenberg's insistence) an outside agency, the Brookings Institution, to resurvey the ground already covered not only by the executive department but also by the Herter Committee and the Foreign Affairs Committee of the House of Representatives.

A good deal of systematic spadework had been done by foreign diplomats in Washington in preparing the State Department, as well as Congress and the public, for what amounted to a continuation of Lend Lease in the postwar period to rebuild the shattered economies of Europe. In this preparation British teamwork was concentrated on the British Loan and Bretton Woods, while the French tended to link loans to the broader continental approach of the Monnet Plan. Effective American channels were as usual the pundits among the columnists, the banking circles (already educated by the Bretton Woods Agreement), and the academic economists who were naturally sympathetic to the needs for world recovery. But the clinching point in carrying the Act through Congress was not economics. It was the realization that this was the only way, short of military action, to fight world communism. The Czechoslovakian coup in February, 1948, clinched this point.

On the American side Congress took the initiative in some sense when, after the Greek-Turkish Aid program and the post-UNRRA emergency aid for Europe in 1947, it demanded that the Administration cease operating in the spasms of crisis, and formulate a total foreign-aid program which could be assessed in terms of a total legislative budget. The size of the national burden—a proper concern of any legislative body exercising the power of the purse—formed the basis of the congressional demand for a coherent "packaged program" on the part of the executive department. The response to this legislative demand for an end to piecemeal aid programs was Under-Secretary of State Acheson's May 8 Mississippi speech and the foreign aid proposal of Secretary Marshall at the Harvard Commencement in June, 1947.

The example of the Economic Cooperation Act, even in such a brief survey of its legislative background, emphasizes the astonishing complexity of American politics, operating not only under foreign pressures but also in the play between the executive and legislative bodies, with a multitude of official instruments operating sometimes tangentially to each other. But the complexity does not stop here. The defeated enemy powers, subsisting on the bounty of the United States (being in some measure stripped of their resources in reparations), introduced another economic factor—but one which had to be filtered through the military chain of command. The clear necessity of protecting and underwriting in a military way the economic recovery of Europe as part of the general struggle against Muscovite communism finally produced the Vandenberg Resolution in the spring of 1948. In rapid succession came the North Atlantic Pact and the Mutual Defense Assistance program for military aid so necessary to supplement economic aid. At the same time, the broad outlines of bipartisan foreign policy, which had somehow been held together in this intragovernmental struggle inside the United States, was subjected to grave and prophetic strains in regard to our policy toward the Far East. The Republican 80th Congress forced on the reluctant Administration more direct and extensive aid to Nationalist China, military and well as economic.

Throughout this entire development, British foreign policy exhibited a remarkable continuity of purpose and directed evolution. Mr. Churchill's role as leader of the Opposition was to press for closer Atlantic union for defense, from the time of his speech at Fulton, Missouri, in 1946, and to give an individual's moral leadership toward establishing closer political and economic union in Europe. In this respect he led the way, even in opposition. His role was constructive. As a critic, he looked beyond the Economic Cooperation Administration, not giving comfort to the Tories who feared dependence on the United States and a partisan advantage for the Labor government.

Moreover, in all the international conferences on the Marshall proposals British representatives, like the British Parliament, showed a remarkable unity of front, a reflection of bipartisan support and disciplined party policy. A single voice and policy was presented to the world by a well-schooled body of negotiators, a marked characteristic of British diplomacy.

On the American side the picture was far less coherent and united. Congressional committees of every kind toured Europe, made investigations, came up with recommendations of varying character. Even within the Executive Branch there were wide divergences over how the program should be organized and where the chief emphasis should fall. More or less clandestine "inspired leaks" through committees on the Hill indicated the dissatisfaction of the Agriculture Department, for example, with the amount of grain to be exported under the Administration's official program. Varying demands for a tougher bargaining position on the part of the United States were reflected in amendments to the Administration bill, as well as in votes on the floor of the House—for example, the vote to include Franco Spain in the aid allotted to Europe (a move voted down in 1948, but passed in 1950).

Yet, ultimately, the Economic Cooperation Administration has been rightly hailed as one of the great constructive bipartisan steps in the history of American foreign policy. It marked the mobilization of overwhelming national support for one of the most generous actions ever taken by a sovereign state. In spite of wide divergences within the executive, within the legislative body, and between them, a reasonably coherent program finally emerged acceptable to the European nations as the basis for cooperation toward their own recovery. It need not, therefore, be argued that lack of professional streamlining in the formation of American policy produced a worse program than would have been achieved by the slicker and aesthetically more satisfying processes of the British system. But to the detached observer, in spite of this successful outcome, the performance of the American system in this critical instance depended in great measure on "accidents"—above all, on the more or less chance personality of Senator Arthur Vandenberg, with his almost unique position in the Republican Party, flanked by such Republicans in the House as Eaton, Dirksen, Herter, and Vorys, among others. Dewey's leadership outside official Washington was also crucial in offsetting Hoover and Taft. Furthermore, the mobilization of popular support depended upon the enlistment of the talents of Secretary of State Acheson, then a private citizen and prime mover in the Citizens' Committee for the Marshall Plan, under the chairmanship of Henry L. Stimson and Robert Patterson. This committee performed something of the same service that the William Allen White Committe had done for Lend Lease Aid to the Allies in the early part of World War II.

The Marshall Plan illustration contains nearly all the elements of the new era of American foreign policy: the emergence of the crucial aspects of economic policy as dominant, the gradual realization of their ultimate relation to basic power and military security, and the new role of Congress as the holder of the purse strings for economic aid and military policy.

Here, too, was developed the new machinery for filtering executive policy first through a series of interdepartmental committees and then through public committees for education and popular support. Finally, there was the pressure of external necessity which produced bipartisan support in adequate measure in both Houses of Congress to achieve a national program. The results look imposing and hopeful. Critics of the machinery of the United States might well be confounded. Popular support was forthcoming.

Yet the real test of the organizational structure was to come when the proportions of the struggle with communism raised the ante for military expenditures and for total foreign aid from 13 billions to over 50 billions, and from 4 billions in annual foreign aid to the 1951 program approximating 8.5 billion dollars. Even these burdens have been accepted; though the end is not yet. A study of the machinery that democracy has produced in the United States to cope with this problem, its relation to the political processes, its strengths and weaknesses, may well be begun by this dramatic introduction to a new era of American foreign policy.

However, the Marshall Plan presented an area of ambiguity or mixed motives. Pressure politics, domestic and foreign, combined to render a type of assistance to Europe less calculated to rebuild a Germany that could be strong against communism and to secure a base of self-help in Europe than to dispose of certain American surpluses, notably agricultural in character. The Administration, moreover, took the easy way in its policy not only toward special interests at home, like shipping, but also toward our allies, with no resort to determined action (for example, dealing on a *quid pro quo* basis) necessary to assure continued United States strength. In spite of sustained and repeated congressional efforts to write into the legislation, against the Administration's wishes, provisions for stockpiling and the long-term development of strategic materials, the executive department proved reluctant to do the difficult job of negotiation which would thus have been imposed. It felt that the Marshall proposals were not a proper subject for "bargaining." Similarly it was not until the German area, particularly in the British Zone, had been very seriously stripped for reparations, by the actual blowing up of buildings as well as by the transfer of machinery, that a congressional injunction to the Executive to negotiate a halt to these proceedings was heeded. Both the failure to take the harder remedy and the reluctance of the Executive to take a lead from Congress that required a tougher attitude toward our allies, as well as toward the Soviets, showed our weaknesses in formulating foreign policy. The weakness of a foreign policy may be far more a matter of what is *not* done than what *is* done. The economic load of the Economic Cooperation Administration might have been greatly lessened had Germany been quickly restored.

Far Eastern policy provided an even more dramatic clash between the Executive and the Legislature and exhibited the lapse of the bipartisan approach. The Republican 80th Congress insisted upon forcing Title IV into the "general package" Economic Cooperation Administration legislation that included military aid to China and a provision for more economic aid than the Administration had originally considered to be desirable or necessary. The deeply felt determination by a majority of at least the lower house of Congress that more aid should be given to the Nationalist regime in China, as well as pressure by a considerable number for more direct military guidance, revealed the fissure between the Administration and considerable sections of the Congress as much as any other area of foreign policy in our postwar history. This rift furnished the emotional background for the congressional reaction to the MacArthur dismissal.

The handicaps to a strong and well-timed policy are many times as serious today, since the United States has taken on responsibilities for conducting international affairs not only through the traditional channels of diplomacy, but also through the multilateral and supranational forum of the United Nations and its specialized agencies. The necessity of doing business with other nations in public assemblies and in a great many specialized agencies imposes a very serious strain on the machinery of coordination—the machinery that depends primarily on smooth relationships between the President and his department heads, between the Executive as a whole and Congress as a whole. Their words and deeds are addressed necessarily to a world audience, no longer just to their own constituents.

America's representatives to the United Nations and its specialized agencies are, furthermore, to some degree independent of any central United States direction and discipline. This is not a deliberate policy of the Executive. It is a logical result of the deficiencies and obscurities within the government as a whole, particularly of the failure of the legislature and the executive to develop a common system of responsibility and discipline. This partial independence also arises from the need to adjust to the necessary "politics" for gaining support for our basic policies in the United Nations, in addition to gaining the support of the Congress of the United States.

SUGGESTED MEANS OF OVERCOMING DIFFICULTIES

In considering the ways and means of meeting these difficulties, we could put no faith in the possibility of creating an ideal system merely by setting up formal devices for consultation between the Executive and the Congress—devices such as an imitation of the parliamentary "question hour," or such as a joint legislative-executive council. Indeed, these devices, by complicating the present informal methods of consultation, might cause even greater difficulties in the process of reaching agreement.

Some more fundamental improvement is clearly needed. But at this point a sharp difference of opinion developed among us. Was the basic fault to be found in the American system of separating powers? Could we find any remedy by modifying our presidental system in the pattern of the British parliamentary system or by some modification of it? We at first split sharply on these issues.

The divergence, interestingly enough, tended to diminish as we discussed the problem, defined more closely our own ideas, and made concessions to the views of others in the light of the facts.

We sought remedial action in three alternative and complementary ways—through basic constitutional reform, through minor structural "tinkering," and through an appeal to more effective leadership.

One view held that our presidential system as it now stands is no longer adequate to conduct this nation safely through the testing times ahead: that is, the paralysis between the Executive and the Legislature requires radical structural changes if this nation is to survive the threat to its security from external sources. Granted that structural changes, no matter how fundamental, cannot alter basic trends; nor can they, for example, reverse the decay of a civilization, if that be in fact the real issue; nor can they insure the survival of a nation which refuses to assess realistically the "power element" in the world. Nevertheless structural changes could make the difference between a workable and an unworkable system to stave off the potentialities of an alleged remedial Caesarism. Such a choice, for such a reason, was a necessity in 1787. Perhaps 1951, like, say, 1785, presents the need for changing an unworkable structure. *Ex post facto* everything looks deterministic, and on such a view there is no room for improvement. However, democratic systems must keep alternatives open. The Founding Fathers in 1787 had an open choice, and they did not in choosing one alternative form of governmental structure foreclose all others forever more. Furthermore their action was taken in a period that must have seemed as threatening as that confronting the nation today.

A second view held that our system does work and will continue to work under the pressure of necessity, through political education and through administrative changes. Lesser administrative and political improvements, entirely possible, would do the trick. To divert attention and energies to "utopian" basic reforms would be to miss the real chance.

A third view was inclined to place less reliance on basic constitutional reform, or on structural tinkering, than on potentialities of better general education and political leadership. The way to get needed discipline into the existing system is through a combination of "events" plus a presidential personality that can enforce discipline by his leadership of public opinion on a recalcitrant Congress, with full backing of the people who have been properly educated to the moral and historical necessities of our foreign policy. There is no substitute for truly great leadership on the part of a President.

CONCESSIONS BY THE OPPONENTS
OF CONSTITUTIONAL REFORM

Those who had at first either opposed the idea of constitutional amendment, or had instead emphasized the need for improvements in administrative procedures or political leadership, tended to concede these points as a result of our discussions:

That administrative reform, or major improvements in the organization and processes of the Executive Branch, could not now go forward as fast as the situation requires without substantial improvements in the organization of the government and in the basic attitudes of its officials, particularly the Congress.

That one major means for producing such improvements would be to strengthen party discipline, so that the majority party in Congress would unite in support of a coherent national policy and would be able to override sectional interests and demands of pressure groups; and that, conversely, a minority party could either unite in support of the administration policy, or develop a clearcut responsible alternative to it.

That the possibility of strengthening party discipline would be greatly enhanced by the adoption of constitutional amendments designed to strengthen the influence of the President as party leader, or to strengthen the two-party system against dissident factions or splinter parties. While we reached no sweeping agreement on all points, there was general approval of the following steps in the form of separate constitutional amendments to strengthen party responsibility:

(1) The nation has now reached the stage where it would be desirable to enact a constitutional amendment which would do away with the sole power of the Senate to approve treaties by a two-thirds vote. We suggest substituting for this present provision the ratification of treaties by an absolute majority of both Houses. This would remove the overweighting of particular blocks of pressure groups and regional interests, given the composition of the Senate. It would also tend to remove any question of legality arising from the present practice of operating in the field of foreign policy through joint resolutions, which have the effect of treaties and yet, under present conditions, are subject to some opposition as an evasion of constitutional provisions. An absolute majority of both

Houses, under present conditions, is unlikely in any way to lessen the protection of legislative sanction for major issues of foreign policy.

(2) We approve of a four-year (instead of the present two-year) term for members of the House of Representatives. This would, in effect, carry the mandate given in presidental elections for a sufficient period to test out a foreign policy and avoid the upsets of the mid-term elections by the calendar, which are generally conceded by students of our political system not to turn on national issues to anything like the degree of presidential elections, since the Presidency is not at stake. Those of us prepared to concede this length of term for the lower House, but who oppose more sweeping amendments (involving, for example, a general election between presidential elections), feel that the very weakness of party discipline would permit a change of sentiment among members of Congress, so that the four-year term would not constitute too great a remove from the check of the elected legislative body on foreign policy.

At the same time, we are all agreed that it would tend to decrease the weight of pressure groups, which now operate with singular effectiveness in the "thinner" voting of the mid-term elections. The position of members of the lower House, perpetually in need of running for nomination and election and of keeping up their "political fences" to the detriment of their national responsibilities, might be greatly improved by this amendment.

(3) The item veto, for appropriation bills at least, and probably to all "money bills," would be a useful strengthening of the President's hand, in the light of our general concern for an increase of executive leadership and power under conditions of world crisis. The President's protection of his budget affecting foreign affairs and defense might be greatly strengthened and the formation of an integrated foreign policy more

readily achieved with the aid of an item veto. Extending the item veto, however, to all legislation would run into difficulties which we have not adequately examined. Therefore, on this generalization of the item veto to *all* legislative enactments we are unwilling to make an agreed proposal.

(4) An amendment to insure the election of the President in a manner that would divide the electoral votes more nearly in terms of the popular vote cast in each state would, we believe, result in distinct improvements. Legally speaking, this is now possible through state laws in each state. But when one state passes a law to throw all its electoral votes as a solid unit to the plurality party in a national election, political weight dictates the same practice to the rest. Uniformity can only be achieved by an amendment to the federal Constitution. Not all of us have examined the proposed Lodge amendment sufficiently to concur in its details, but we are all prepared to support the general principle incorporated in it. Decreasing the power of minority blocks in the large states would be eminently desirable. These minority groups, particularly in great cities, throw undue weight in presidential elections at the present time, since they may determine the delivery of many electoral votes by a narrow majority in states like New York, Pennsylvania, Illinois, California, and Ohio. Our national policy certainly does not suffer from too little representation of racial or religious or nationality minorities. An amendment to prevent the choice of major party candidates from falling as it does at present almost entirely to citizens of the very large states would greatly increase the range of available talents for the most difficult office in modern times—the Presidency of the United States. In general, such an amendment would increase the factors making for choice along national lines and on the broadest basis and decrease the weighting of minorities in big cities and of candidates who are prepared to court these minorities.

(5) We are generally sympathetic toward an amendment which would permit some form of "packing" each House with a number of Cabinet members or other heads of agencies chosen at the President's discretion. As this proposal rose rather late in our discussions, we feel a proper reluctance to pass judgment on such a sweeping amendment and prefer rather to emphasize the need for further study to determine its full implications. Such details as these deserve careful consideration: What would be an appropriate number (ten was suggested for the Senate and twenty for the House); what would be the privileges for the members of the Executive in Congress; what would be the rights of Congress to call on members of the Executive for information in open session or on demand; and what ultimately would be the psychological effect on the relations between Congress and the Executive? It does seem to us that this proposal might have real merit. It could help to bridge the gap between Executive and Legislative Branches. It could further weight the importance of national elections and put a premium on shaping them toward the decision of great issues of national policy. But it needs more study.

In addition to these five generally agreed changes, some discussion was given to the more sweeping proposal for adding some form of the general election device to our constitutional system, in a way that would permit the President to break what he considered to be a dangerous or hopeless deadlock confronting his paramount policies by calling a general election at least once during his term and for at least the membership of the lower House. It was agreed, however, that there was too little consensus to press discussion of this controversial proposal.

While there was agreement, then, on the desirability of certain constitutional amendments, there was no such unanimity as to the urgency or practicability of making such changes. Some of us feel that we have not the time in this period of crisis to divert energies from substantive policy to controversial "reforms." Others urge that without basic reforms the drift toward Caesarism might become a real danger, should our system fail to meet adequately and in time the challenge of totalitarian attack in all its forms. We signal this point because of its close relationship to the difficulties experienced by Woodrow Wilson and by many other Presidents in achieving disciplined support for commitments which were worse than useless when not supported by the nation.

CONCESSIONS BY THE PROPONENTS OF CONSTITUTIONAL REFORM

Those of us who started out with an emphasis on institutional handicaps, who thought, for example, that only a constitutional amendment giving the President power to dissolve the Congress (and submit his tenure with that of the Congress to the vote of the people) would make it possible to increase the responsibility of political parties for government-wide policy, tended to concede the following points during subsequent discussions:

(1) That the proper working of a parliamentary system (as in the United Kingdom and the British Dominions) depended not only on the device of dissolution to settle major disputes between the Legislature and the Executive (although dissolution is an essential cog in the machinery), but also on a concentration of power within the Legislature, so that a single House could override the other House of the Legislature, and so that no committee of the principal House could block the policy of the majority party within that House.

(2) That the United States, if it should adopt a constitutional amendment to permit appeal to the electorate in case of disagreement between the President and the Congress, ought to give the power of dissolution to the President alone, and not to the Congress; so that the choice of a time for a new

election might be made with due regard for factors in foreign and military policy on which it would not be practicable to keep a majority of the Congress always fully informed.

(3) That those interested in the improvement of the government's ability to deal with foreign policy should not abstain from more limited efforts in order to concentrate on constitutional reform, since, for one thing, the historical development of the United States has so strongly embedded the traditional pattern that the likelihood of a basic overhaul of the Constitution is perhaps not more likely than the development of the pattern of Caesarism.

(4) That, also, bipartisan support for foreign policies, even in the parliamentary system, has tended to overshadow party discipline in order to insure broad general support and continuity for foreign policy. In times of national peril this habit of mature democracies could in general be relied on to overcome ordinary legislative blocks.

REMAINING AREA OF DISAGREEMENT

However these concessions did not entirely eliminate our disagreement on the best means of overcoming difficulties precipitated by the doctrine of separation of powers.

On the one hand, some still maintained that the only way to increase party responsibility and to strengthen the hand of the President at critical moments, when his program is endangered by combinations of pressure groups and sectional interests acting without regard for national interests, was to adopt a constitutional amendment—an amendment which would make a radical change in the relations between the Executive and Legislative Branches, giving the President the right to call a general election once during his term at his discretion. Only such a dramatic national election, it was argued, could increase party discipline and make the representatives less dependent on local issues.

On the other hand, others maintained with equal conviction that the primary difficulty was within the Congress, or in the relations of Congressmen to their constituents. The device of dissolution, they countered, would be unlikely to persuade the Congress to give up its specialized committees or its habits of working for constituents. And any campaign to change the constitutional provision regarding the election of the President and the Congress might result in giving Congress the power in effect to elect and dismiss the President—which would be fatal to the degree of party and administrative discipline which the nation now has.

It was agreed at least that if such sweeping constitutional change were to be attempted, it had better be undertaken through the calling of a national convention than by the alternative procedure which would originate in the Congress itself.

OTHER REFORMS

Leaving this degree of disagreement in the record for others to ponder and perhaps resolve, we turned to consider what could be done within the present constitutional framework to lessen the difficulties that have been caused by building into the organization of the Executive Branch and into the procedures of Congress an unconscionable quantity of checks and balances through statutory enactment and custom.

A MORE EFFECTIVE *modus vivendi* BETWEEN THE PRESIDENT AND CONGRESS

Short of constitutional reform, it seems indispensable to develop a more effective *modus videndi* between the President and Congress. The best way to do this in the long run probably would be to raise the general level of political education and leadership. In the short run, the situation would be helped by an improvement in the techniques of consultation and cooperation between the Executive and Legislative Branches.

The natural obstacles (other than those arising from the lack of a basic organization of mutual responsibility) to effective executive cooperation with Congress are threefold: ignorance, ill will, honest disagreement. Ignorance as a factor in executive cooperation with Congress can be remedied by improving the flow of information to Congress by consultation, liaison, social evenings, etc. But there are limits to the efficiency of consultation and liaison. People cannot be made to believe what they do not want to believe. Moreover, the time factor limits the energy which important officials in the Executive Branch can devote to Congress. Is it more important for Lovett to improve our defenses, Wilson to mobilize our industry, Acheson to strengthen our foreign policy? Or is it more important for them to spend days in endless testimony before congressional committees? It is sometimes hard to do both.

Ill will presents a different problem: here is included not just personal malevolence, but that conception of party politics which holds that the duty of the opposition is to oppose, whatever the time, place, or issue. A Senator who opposes the Administration in principle creates a problem of non-collaboration which in normal times can be solved only by retiring the Senator (or the Administration). In times of crisis, however, the belief in opposition is likely to be overridden (on the surface, at least) by other considerations. Thus nearly every isolationist member of Congress pledged his undying support to the war effort on December 8, 1941; though a few months later many of them had set up business again at the same old stand. Some were, indeed, retired.

The more basic issue, however, is how to handle honest disagreement over the course required by the national interest.

This is a divergence of understanding and of political values, rather than a defect in the system of consultative contrivances which is likely to be at the base of a really serious stalemate between Congress and the White House.

In the last decade Colonel Lindbergh, Colonel McCormick, Herbert Hoover, and Henry Wallace have argued in various contexts that the totalitarianization of Europe would present no serious threat to the United States. These are mature men with convictions not likely to be reversed in an evening's argument, nor by any amount of liaison and consultation. The attempt to educate them to the Administration's analysis and evaluation is likely to be futile. Much better is it to try to educate the people who might otherwise be persuaded by them.

The decisive factor—the solvent (or the preventative) of the previous stalemates in our history has been real political leadership. The great Presidents have always "had the drop" on Congress because in moments of crisis they could appeal over the head of Congress to the people. The present situation calls for a far more effective, systematic and sustained attempt to explain to the Congress and the people the moral and historical necessities behind our foreign policy. They must be convinced.

PRIOR CONGRESSIONAL APPROVAL OF MAJOR SHIFTS IN THE NATION'S MILITARY POSTURE

The general relationship of military and political problems was a theme of discussion recurring at nearly every part of our inquiry. Our general conclusions on the subject are stated below (pages 107–13, 161–62, and 198–200), but one special aspect of the matter deserves consideration here. One of the recurrent areas of struggle between the Congress and the Executive is the contest over their respective war powers. No prescription can end this contest, since both parties have clear-cut constitutional rights which overlap. It is our feeling, however, that the following propositions could and should command support on both sides:

(1) That a state of war requires a devolution on the Executive of very large discretionary power, whose outstanding characteristic is that it can be ended by the Legislature at any time. The Legislature also, of course, should sit regularly and criticize freely, but responsibly.

(2) That the Congress may always repudiate any major shift in military posture and, whatever may be the wisdom of such a repudiation, there can be no denial of the constitutional rights of Congress in this connection. Unless there are pressing grounds of urgency or secrecy, there are major advantages in prior congressional approval of such major shifts.

(3) That between peace and war there are many stages within each of which the Chief Executive requires and must be granted a considerable freedom of action, just as in all-out war the Commander in Chief must be given extraordinary powers.

MORE WISDOM, BETTER COORDINATION, BETTER PERSONNEL, BETTER FINANCING AND MORE AUTHORITY

Imbedded in the whole operation of government, apart from the separation of powers, is a lack of certain essentials not necessarily related to the mechanics of the problem. It is not enough to tie the structure together at the top. It is necessary to tie it together all the way "down and up." If a government is ever to be coordinated, it must be coordinated in the minds of the people who authorize it and those who operate it, from the top to the bottom of the structure. Moreover, a solution requires not just better coordination of structural changes, but also better personnel, better financing, and more authority from the public to conduct foreign relations. This is not a demand for perfection, but it is the necessary direction for any progress.

III

THE ROLE OF EXECUTIVE

ORGANIZATION

OBSERVATIONS ON THE ROLE OF THE PRESIDENT
IN FOREIGN POLICY

ONE OF THE important shortcomings in the formation and conduct of United States foreign policy is the lack of what, for want of a better word, is often called "coordination" at the national level. The Executive has to have both concentrated authority and concentrated responsibility in order to formulate and carry out foreign policy. The government of the United States possesses neither of these attributes.

Efforts to improve the Executive in structure and function have been concentrated during the last two decades on the way in which the President organizes and supervises subordinates. Much less attention has been devoted to the problem of working out the relationship between Congress, on the one hand, and the President and the Executive Branch, on the other, so that they can work more cooperatively on high-level issues. The top administrative personnel is not a unifying force in support of executive leadership. It is divided into various corps; it has little continuity of service; its loyalties run to various departments (and their corresponding pressure groups), rather than to the government as a whole.

The "powers" of the President have grown, but there are great restrictions on his administrative influence: while party leadership and patronage have weakened, the government has grown so large that the President can control it administratively only through institutional staffing—and that can be provided only in the numbers, and according to the terms, decided by Congress. On the other hand, the President has these advantages: he is elected directly for a fixed term of office, and he is the chief of state as well as the head of administration and the leader of the dominant party. Consequently, he can normally appeal to the public (including members of both parties) to accept policies that may be at the moment unacceptable to the congressional leadership of either party. This gives him a bargaining position as the national leader which is the main force for cohesion in a loosely coordinated system. He must win backing from his own party to be safe. But in foreign policy he needs majority support by both parties.

Not only is the President handicapped by the lack of coordination on foreign policy, but he must now carry a larger personal burden on its substantive issues. For example, military policy, particularly in the area of "national interest," is now such an integral part of foreign affairs that control of foreign policy is of necessity lifted from the departmental to the presidential level. In acknowledging final presidential authority, one must at the same time acknowledge the logic of coordination by the State Department with respect to many phases of foreign policy, and acknowledge also a need for the maintenance of machinery with which to settle most foreign policy issues at subordinate levels. Furthermore, it is necessary to recognize the important new role of the Secretary of Defense in the formulation and conduct of a national policy which must be based both on the dynamics of persuasion and on the dynamics of force.

A review of the constitutional position and historic practices of the President and the Congress would illustrate the tremendous growth of executive discretion in the conduct of foreign policy and in the setting of conditions, military and psychological, which control the most important issues of foreign relations, including war. It would illustrate also the pressure which the Executive has felt to associate with him appropriate congressional leadership, both formally and informally, in the formative stages of foreign policy. It is both politically necessary and intrinsically good democratic policy for the Executive to have congressional support in the important matter of the use of armed force. It shows, as well, that even though the President may act by executive agreement to conclude many types of negotiations which have the force of treaties, he has been impelled by the need for congressional support to pursue the device of ratification by joint resolution or by mere legislative enactment, as was the case with the Economic Cooperation Administration program. Furthermore, the Executive has on occasion been influenced by strongly felt legislative attitudes on foreign relations formally announced through congressional resolutions. But such resolutions, even without official policy status, more often serve simply the useful functions of letting off pressure that might otherwise become dangerous, thus guiding the Executive as to the sentiment of the country.

SUGGESTED REFORMS IN THE PRESIDENT'S ROLE

There is no substitute for truly great leadership on the part of the President in the formulation and conduct of foreign policy. No one but the President can do this central job. Charles A. Beard's well-known definition of a statesman indicates the desideratum; we acknowledge this through feeling the inspiration of the great men who have fulfilled the concept, not only in the contemporary public mind but also in the early struggle for the nation's survival and during its subsequent growth and testing. "A statesman," said the late Charles A. Beard, "is one who sees the long future, the place of his nation and himself in it; who labors diligently on behalf of his countrymen; has courage; takes risks; has a certain amount of luck; and goes off the stage with a reasonable degree of dignity."

Short of innate, truly great leadership on the part of a President, there is still no substitute for active, direct and decisive presidential control. This conclusion, painful as it may be to those who put faith in fool-proof organization charts when they have no faith in the Chief Executive *per se,* has about it the comforting ring of realism. As voters, we all tend to recognize the critical importance of the presidential election; there is no reason why, as students, we should rate it less lightly. If we conclude that the President himself is the key figure in policy and defense, we are well in line with the basic premises of our constitutional system. The President today probably carries a greater weight of responsibility than the Founding Fathers foresaw. But is it useful, or "scientific," in any real sense to conceal this responsibility in blueprints, councils, committees, and the like?

The President must take counsel of his experts; he must act through his duly constituted agencies, wherever possible; he must, in any event, keep them fully informed. But he cannot delegate; rather he must actively exercise his own basic power of decision and direction. In the nature of the case, if he does not do it, no one else can; and in the nature of the present case, it must be done. This one of the "facts of life" in terms of political realities helps to explain why the Presidency is such a killing job—yet one which still finds, happily, willing aspirants for the prospectively fatal honor.

No changes in the attitude and purpose of any part of the Executive Branch can change the personality of a President. The Executive Branch—and the President himself—must "make do" with what the voters have provided. With this exception, however, there is extraordinary latitude for change, at the word of the President and without fear of congressional opposition, along the lines here suggested. For example, President Truman has it in his power to assist and press the Department of State a long way in its recent attempts to escape from "diplomacy" and "principles" of a pale and negative sort. He has it in his power, if he chooses to use it as his own highest council, to make the National Security Council a true policy cabinet, not a sifter of staff memoranda; he can insure and perhaps even fix for good, if he is lucky, a properly high concept of the Secretary of Defense. There is nothing inevitable (though under our system there is much that is "natural") in the picture, now so familiar, of a divided Administration, a negative State Department, and a self-sufficient Defense Establishment. Granted that the picture has been much improved from what it was even a brief year ago, the central argument here is simply that principle and opportunity combine to urge a still more sweeping and much more rapid adjustment to a world in which only bold, expert, forceful politics can safeguard our survival.

WHAT CONSTITUTES EFFECTIVE EXECUTIVE INTEGRATION OF POLICY?

A large part of our discussion necessarily revolved about the relations of policy-making to organization and particularly to administration. Integration of policy for the Executive Branch must of necessity center in the President of the United States, and for that reason in the Executive Office of the President, since the Executive Office furnishes him with his own staff. How can his own personal "span of control" be combined with good administration? Deferring an analysis of the details of this problem as they relate to the several layers of executive staff organization already apparent in the White House and in the extensions of the Executive Office, we believe it useful to point out as a framework of reference for any fruitful study the following prerequisites of good administration:

(1) The first necessity of any organizational problem is to understand *what are* the objectives; in other words, to frame the right questions for policy in order to delimit areas of responsibility and to work out at appropriate levels an effective machinery for decision-making and for follow-through. This means high-level staff analysis and the capacity of an executive to understand and use it.

(2) In the area of foreign policy the new range of problems affecting the entire life of a nation has required the development of entirely new staff concepts for policy formulation and control in attempting to find an answer to the problem of whose is the primary responsibility for decision. In so far as responsibility can be clearly fixed on a department without necessity for more than consultation with the other interested agencies, a sound principle of administration has been achieved. But it is increasingly clear that in areas affecting economics and military security, as well as political support in a democracy by huge segments of the population, consultation is not enough. The staff functions of the President must insure clearance with agencies who are vitally concerned with solutions, in order to establish that their interests have been adequately taken into account in the formation of national policy. In its simplest form this can be seen in the necessity for clearing speeches involving important statements on national policy. Cables and instructions to the field ordinarily have the same problem of clearance.

(3) The third level is to secure decision where major disagreement exists between agencies with no clear authority within any one of them to settle an issue involving two or more. The creation of the National Security Council is a dramatic highlight of an interdepartmental structure which had already achieved considerable proportions in the National Advisory

Council on international monetary and financial policy and other instances. Setting up a board of advisers to the chairman of every major war agency which included representatives of the affected departments was intended to fix in the structures created during World War II a model that would secure at least consultation. This model has been widely followed, as, for instance, in the Defense Mobilization Board and the National Security Resources Board. But the adjustment of inter-agency disputes carries far beyond the limits of possible decision-making of the Budget Bureau and even of such presidential agencies as the Office of Defense Mobilization. The President himself is confronted with inevitable differences of opinion between members of his Cabinet and his own staff, for which the Cabinet meetings afford no adequate point of resolution. It is in this area that his White House assistants and his extended staff machinery are brought to play.

Decision-making, as between the major agencies of the government, can hardly stop short of the President himself; though the issues may be clarified and presented to him by adequate staff work. In certain areas he has found it necessary to set up a Special Assistant like Mr. Harriman, or a Director like Mr. Wilson, responsible for all agencies involved in defense mobilization, with a view to settling disputes short of the President himself, in so far as possible. But even at this high level of presidential staff, no finality of decision can be expected where Cabinet members with direct access to the President are involved.

(4) Where lines of administration have been, as far as possible, clearly organized so as to get effective and quick decisions on matters of vital policy, there remains the necessity to achieve the most important part of good administration, namely, the selection of the right men. Since administration can hardly be better than the understanding of the problems on which it is based, the ability to analyze with understanding

is crucial. But beyond that, it goes without saying that force and leadership, a just weighing of the opinions of subordinates, and an ability to organize, to devolve and to hold together are all parts of the ideal administrator. The weakness of our government in not being able to hold many of the best men in public office may be its greatest fault, whatever the reasons.

It is only in this light that organizational charts and systematic framework for securing lines of responsibility and follow-up can be understood. There is a technique of administration, but it all rests upon the caliber of the men who do it and the character of the policies which they are to carry out.

OBSERVATIONS ON THE EXECUTIVE OFFICE OF THE PRESIDENT

If the President is to coordinate the Executive Branch, Congress must let him have the machinery to do so. To be sure, the President has been given such support in some measure at least. But only a little more than a dozen years ago this was not true. The Executive Office of the President was not created until 1939; the White House Office, for fear of congressional disapproval, was until 1945 staffed mainly by subterfuge—that is, by borrowing personnel from various departments. Since that time the Congress has not only continued to support the Executive Office, in which the Budget Bureau is probably the most important single agency; it has also given the President new staff agencies. It set up the Council of Economic Advisers in the Executive Office by statute, and it approved reorganization plans transferring to the Executive Office the National Security Council and the National Security Resources Board. More recently there has been added the Office of Defense Mobilization, with perhaps (on paper) the broadest grant of delegated authority ever made by any Chief Executive. But it is generally agreed that the President needs even more institutional assistance than he now has to help him to coordinate the departments, especially through the Executive Office and through high-level interdepartmental committees.

SUGGESTED REFORMS IN THE EXECUTIVE OFFICE OF THE PRESIDENT

GENERAL REMEDIES

The first step in improving the conduct of foreign policy is to get the executive house in order—to see that the executive agencies operating in foreign affairs act in unity. This problem can only be dealt with; it can never be solved. It may be dealt with by such devices of coordination as interdepartmental committees at various levels, including top-level coordinating bodies like the National Security Council; by the use of the individual staff members of the President in the White House; and by the institutional staff in the rest of the Executive Office. All of these devices require support, adjustment, and constant interposition by the President. The inherent difficulty in executive staff work is that no formal device can transcend the will (or wit) of those who make it work—including not only the executive officials themselves, but all those whose support is required in a democracy for the conduct of public business.

Even if the United States government can make all the adjustments in structures and organization that are needed, the officials concerned will still need to acquire more of a common outlook and more recognition of their obligation to develop and support a responsible government-wide policy. If the diffusion of formal responsibility in the conduct of foreign affairs cannot, or should not, be avoided, then it is equally important to try to permeate this disjointed machinery with a common viewpoint. Some of us think that this may be done through the techniques developed by the secretariats of the Cabinet and by the various committees in the British

government, and through the addition of something else which
the British do not have and do not need: a formal centralized
system of in-service training, as well as the exchange of views
and the development of common ideas among all government
officials, executive and legislative, who have responsibility for
the conduct of foreign affairs. Others are skeptical of any
formal system for this purpose, even though they agree on the
great need for the development of a central theoretical approach to foreign policy questions which could be disseminated
to the great number of government officials whose activities
bear in some way or another on American foreign policy.

STAFF COORDINATION

The President cannot do the whole coordinating job from
his own office. He must use agencies in the Executive Office,
and especially individual assistants in the White House, but
only to deal with those problems which should not be assigned
to operating departments. Almost every department has some
responsibility for coordinating the activities of others on one
type of problem or another. In the supremely important field
of foreign affairs the Department of State must play a primary
and even dominant role, and the Secretary of State must act
as the President's agent in developing and coordinating government-wide programs.

Nevertheless, the new intensity and range of foreign policy,
its extensive impact on our domestic economy and the political
system, and the obligations assumed under the United Nations
Charter require the President to use his Executive Office to
supplement the efforts of the Department of State.

This requirement arises in part from the need for the President's political leadership, since foreign affairs create, or involve, political issues which are beyond the influence and
management of the Secretary of State. And this results in the
further necessity of developing a more effective staff at the

White House for dealing with Congress, especially to maintain liaison and provide information for individual Congressmen as voting issues arise. If overdone, this kind of work is attacked as executive pressure on the legislative process. But it is also possible to do so little of it that Congressmen who otherwise might well be glad to follow the general Administration policy are left uninformed.

A second type of staff work needed by the President can be done only by men of great ability and influence who can serve as individual staff assistants to help him coordinate executive policies. Among the considerable number of presidential assistants at the present time, two are worth particular attention in connection with foreign affairs. One is the Special Assistant to the President (Mr. W. Averell Harriman). With the aid of a small staff, he helps the President handle particularly difficult interdepartmental problems affecting foreign affairs. The other is Director of the Office of Defense Mobilization (Mr. Charles E. Wilson), to whom the President has delegated very sweeping decision-making powers regarding industrial mobilization as it relates to national and international defense. Both Mr. Harriman and Mr. Wilson are regularly invited to attend the meetings of the National Security Council.*

Presidential assistants—whether their jobs have been created simply by presidential order or have been set up by statute—depend for influence and authority on the continuous support of the President. The boundaries of their influence cannot be discovered merely by reading the language of the orders which created them, for those boundaries are so broad

---

* The new Mutual Security Aid law passed by Congress in September, 1951, imposes new duties of an executive order on a Director of Mutual Security, who is to be Mr. Harriman. This changes his function to one carrying responsibilities like those of the Director of the Office of Defense Mobilization, as well as his previous staff duties on a policy level. This act also carries statutory membership for the Director of Mutual Security on the National Security Council. No comment is possible on Mr. Wilson's resignation (April, 1952).

as to overlap each other's and the functions of other parts of
the Executive Office, as well as those of many of the operating
departments. Moreover, these presidential assistants do not
have the support that an executive department acquires by
performing functions for a large clientele that may be influential
with public opinion and with the Congress. The problem
results as to how to set up such presidential assistants in a way
that will enable them to work most effectively with other parts
of the Executive Office and with the operating departments.
The more such assistants can operate as agents of the President,
and the less they have to take responsibility publicly for acting
against the interests of the operating departments, the more
durable and useful they are likely to be. In emergencies, however, it may be necessary—as it was considered necessary in
setting up the Office of Defense Mobilization—to grant conspicuous power and authority to a presidential assistant; such
status may give him much greater opportunity for service to
the President, even though it may make him, in the end,
politically expendable.

Some difficult problems arise from the very fact that the
President has such extensive staff assistance in the Executive
Office. In addition to Mr. Harriman and Mr. Wilson, there are
a number of White House staff members and several Executive
Office agencies (the National Security Council, the National
Security Resources Board, and the Bureau of the Budget)—
all with important roles in the conduct of foreign affairs. In this
multiplicity there is no single effective center in the White
House where policy can be coordinated with consideration of
domestic politics. There is no single point, besides the President himself, where one can go for action on issues which cut
across the present functional divisions within the Executive
Office.

We agreed that there was need for considerably greater
unity within the operations of the Executive Office itself. For

this purpose it seemed clearly desirable for the President to reduce considerably the number of persons within the Executive Office who deal directly with him on issues relating to foreign affairs. One opinion within the Group carried this idea further in recommending that the President place some one subordinate—be he an Assistant President or a Secretary of State, or the head of some new Cabinet office—firmly and emphatically above everyone else in the Executive Branch in all matters of external affairs. Such an official would have to be given great authority to make final decisions and to resolve the innumerable differences of interest and outlook which boil within official Washington.

A less drastic action would be to set up within the Executive Office some type of chief of staff who would not have direct authority over the operating departments, but who would be used by the President to coordinate (with authority) the staff work within the Executive Office itself. One possibility would be to use the Budget Bureau Director for this purpose, since that official is in charge of the oldest and largest agency in the Executive Office, the one which has the most general function, and the one which has come closest to developing a strong tradition of non-political staff work. He is equipped, too, with an existing staff arm that, with improvement in personnel and methods, could really furnish "eyes and ears" and a check-up on performance.

There was support, too, for the idea that the President should always be reluctant to have any subordinate in a position strong enough to develop by any means a policy independent of the President's—by statutory authority, by administrative routine, or by the manipulation of publicity. The President should always insist on dealing directly with all members of his Cabinet on major operating issues, and with the several top officials within his Executive Office for advice and staff work. If this were so, he might still use some kind of "staff coordinator" or "staff secretary" in the Executive Office —an officer, that is, who would have the general assignment of helping the President to cordinate the Executive Office activities, but no formal authority, no responsibility for policy decisions, and no public role of his own. However, the ordinary White House assistants and staff should never be interposed as a reviewing layer with authority to make policy decisions or act on their own.

INTERDEPARTMENTAL COMMITTEES

The Executive Office, of course, cannot coordinate the Executive Branch by settling every point on which its departments disagree. It would be physically impossible to manage the Executive Branch if the departments did not get together to develop some kind of teamwork at working levels up and down the line. As foreign and domestic policy have come more and more to depend upon each other, the Executive Branch has come more and more to rely on the use of interdepartmental committees for purposes of coordination.

These committees must be related in the proper manner to the use of executive authority and to the use of executive staff work. Minor interdepartmental committees, as well as the Cabinet itself, will be most useful if the President can keep their assignments flexible and their deliberations confidential, and if he can use his special assistants or other staff to help committee members rise above their departmental interests. It has been suggested, for example, that the Special Assistant to the President (Mr. Harriman) should, in the President's absence from meetings of the National Security Council, act as his deputy to serve as chairman of the meetings. The purpose of this arrangement would be to enable the Secretary of State to speak more freely as advocate of his department's policies than he can do while serving as chairman. Whether or not this arrangement would be effective depends, of course, on the personal relationships between the President and his Special Assistant, and between the Special Assistant and the Cabinet members concerned, particularly State and Defense.

Perhaps the greatest difficulty in the use of interdepartmental committees has come from trying to make them do things for which they are completely unsuited.

First of all, such committees cannot bring about agreement between departments if each of the departments concerned does not know its own mind. Before any of our present committees can operate satisfactorily, each of the departments which participate in them needs to be tightened up, so that its head can be made more fully responsible for its operations, and so that any of his subordinates who takes part in committee work can speak with confidence in stating the policy of his superior.

Next, the committees need to learn how to relate their work to general executive policy. Whether the interdepartmental committee is useful, or whether it compounds confusion, depends on how it is used. It depends, to be specific, on whether these several committees are thought of as agents of the President's management, or whether they are thought of as little independent islands of quasi-legislative authority within the Executive Branch. There must be an effective chairman, as well as an alert and able secretariat. Generally, power to act for any committee with the exception of the National Security Council should be vested in the chairman.

If each committee considers that it has acquired a corporate personality and an independent reason for existence, the result will be chaos. For the decision on a hard problem will not then depend on a responsible policy of the Administration. Rather it will depend on the personal manipulations of the chairmen. In such an event, responsibility would be hopelessly obscured, and nobody would gain. Yet the only way to avoid this is to stand by the constitutional theory that power to act should be vested by law in the President and the individual heads of executive departments, and coordination of their policies should be left to his discretion. If Congress by law determines the membership and jurisdiction of coordinating committees, those committees will immediately lose their usefulness to the President and will become authoritative operating agencies which themselves will be unable to coordinate with anything else.*

The same general theory which governs the use of staff agencies should apply to interdepartmental committees: they should serve the Executive, not merely usurp a part of his power, without responsibility for its effective exercise. Congress sometimes sets them up as if they were responsible to Congress or could act alone, even though the saving clause "under the direction of the President" is inserted in the law authorizing the agencies.

Admittedly, we cannot make our coordinating machinery work well just by having the Congress leave it alone. And in the work of the Cabinet committees and interdepartmental committees it presently appears that an opportunity is being missed. Most of them have their own independent secretariats, each of which, consequently, has a jurisdictional motive for competing with the others. Some central management by the President's Executive Office is required to supplement what he can do personally by his regular meetings with the most important Cabinet committees. The National Security Council offers a nucleus and an opportunity, with a focus of general importance.

* This difficulty has arisen in a serious way in the National Security Council for which Congress enacted its statutory membership. Congress cannot, of course, constitutionally prevent the President adding others to the National Security Council deliberations when he seeks advice. Still there is a tendency to vie for one of the statutory posts and to feel less strong in argument if the agency is not so nominated.

THE NATIONAL SECURITY COUNCIL

A discussion of the Executive Office of the President would hardly be complete without taking special note of the National Security Council. The essential problems which give rise to such top-level coordinating Cabinet committees emerge from factors which have also led to such roles as those played by W. Averell Harriman, both before and since his acceptance of the new duties as Mutual Security Administrator (October, 1951); by Harry Hopkins in the preceding Roosevelt Administration, and, on the economic side of similar problems where foreign policy and domestic policy come together, by the functioning of Mr. Justice Byrnes's Office of War Mobilization and Reconversion (well described in Herman Somers's *Presidential Agency*); and now the Office of Defense Mobilization under Charles E. Wilson. One might possibly add the Psychological Strategy Board, first under President Gray and now under President Allen. The Central Intelligence Agency also serves several departments and must collect, digest, and interpret all types of intelligence.

The National Security Council is in reality an interdepartmental committee, with staff, designed by its review and advice to the President to bring unity, or at the least coordination, into the policy actions which seriously affect our national security. Its activity centers on the Departments of State, Defense, Treasury, the National Security Resources Board, the Office of Defense Mobilization, the Mutual Security Administration, and some other agencies. For this reason there is always a possible overlap with other parts of the Executive Office of the President, such as those formerly exercised by Mr. Harriman as Special Assistant and Mr. Wilson in the Office of Defense Mobilization and by the Bureau of the Budget. The President presides personally over the National Security Council and makes all official decisions by his own order. He presides also (with Mr. Wilson as Deputy Chairman) over the Defense Mobilization Advisory Board. But that body is not interdepartmental, and no orders issue from it. It is a public, rather than an official, advisory committee. By contrast the proceedings and decisions of the National Security Council are at all stages protected by the highest degree of secrecy.

The question naturally arises as to whether the National Security Council should or could become the major regular method of resolving at the highest level, short of the President's personal decision, difficulties of an interagency character (including other Executive Office agencies) on domestic as well as foreign and military issues that affect national security; or whether the President would be better advised to avoid any fully defined jurisdictional finality or responsibility among his own top staff officials.

The scope of this Report has not permitted description of a detailed nature. Nevertheless the difficulty of getting adequate information on the working of the National Security Council and the make-up and character of its staff calls for an outline at least of its present functions and evolution since its creation by the National Security Act of 1947 (amended in 1949). The establishment of this Council was the result of studies conducted for Secretary Forrestal by a committee under the direction of Ferdinand Eberstadt. This Eberstadt study was certainly influenced by British experience with the Committee of Imperial Defense, called the Defense Committee after World War II. Indeed, Lord Hankey furnished the study committee under Eberstadt with one of the few detailed accounts ever written down of the make-up and functions of the Committee of Imperial Defense.

The need for better alignment of foreign policy to defense had been recognized in Britain at least since the time of the Esher Committee. The Committee of Imperial Defense was created to remedy the gross inadequacies of the Empire's defense planning and machinery which were shown by the Boer War. An additional factor in its creation, lacking in the United States, was the desire to find some form of high-level "inner Cabinet" agency into which the self-governing Dominions might be introduced as participants, though hardly as full partners. But the following basic reasons that led Lord Balfour in 1904 to set up the Committee of Imperial Defense also applied to this country:

(1) The necessary correlation between effective military power and commitments or alliances in foreign policy had become painfully evident to the British by that time.

(2) Since Britain, like the United States, did not represent a power whose military striking force could ever be decisive in land engagements at the outset of a war, systematic plans for the most rapid possible mobilization of all resources of the Empire, including manpower, had to be worked out in advance.

(3) There was recognition, too, of the need for a continuous method of permitting the Prime Minister or his trusted deputy to resolve differences among the fighting services and the Foreign Office, the Treasury, the Colonial Office, and the India Office, secretly and without airing them even before the entire Cabinet.

(4) An adequate balance between civilian control and military expertise was also a primary aim of the new committee. Balfour himself felt that by assuring this combination he had made the most original and important contribution to Britain's future defense needs.

(5) Finally, staff work on the basis of joint participation by all the services and agencies could be brought continuously to bear in *foreseeing* contingencies which would arise, both in the light of present commitments in foreign policy and of possible hostilities.

Out of the organization of the Committee of Imperial Defense came the War Cabinet and the permanent Cabinet

Secretariat. Lloyd George reveals this in his *Memoirs* in describing a memorable conversation in the Garden of Versailles with Sir Maurice (now Lord) Hankey in 1916. This adaptation was to provide the flexibility of an inner Cabinet of five or six members to operate in times of great crisis, supported by excellent staff work at all times. This experiment in fact has conditioned the whole subsequent development of British top-level organization, in war and in peace.

No similar experiments proved possible in the United States, quite apart from the difference in the character and tradition of the two Cabinets. In the first place, the relationship of power to policy was never clearly accepted, as has been emphasized in this Report. Either the President allowed a dominant Secretary of State like Charles Evans Hughes to settle these issues; or he let them go in some measure by default, as happened under the Coolidge Administration; or he acted in effect as his own Secretary of State, of War, and of Navy, as Franklin D. Roosevelt did. As a result, as was brought out in the Pearl Harbor hearings, this country had only a very casual and somewhat informal type of meetings of the Secretaries of State, War, and Navy. Moreover, Mr. Roosevelt definitely turned down the idea of a defense council on a regular basis, as had been proposed to him by Bernard Baruch and many others. During World War II it is interesting that the President preferred to set up Admiral Leahy as a sort of personal Chief of Staff in his own immediate White House entourage and to run the foreign policy of the country not so much through the State Department as through Harry Hopkins and through his own high-level decisions taken with Churchill and eventually with Stalin.

Now it is true that the President can never delegate his responsibility for top decisions. This is recognized by both the statutory basis and the actual practice of the National Security

Council, which make that body *advisory* to the President. Indeed the advice which reaches the President from the National Security Council may come to him in terms of a clear split on policy among the agencies concerned.

What advantages does the National Security Council then offer and what are some of its present difficulties?

Set up as it is, with the Secretary of State, Secretary of Defense, the Chairman of the National Security Resources Board as well as the Chairman of the Joint Chiefs of Staff, and now the Director for Mutual Security as regular statutory members and with the Director of the Central Intelligence reporting to agencies concerned through the Council, the question immediately arose as to the President's right to appoint other members. Undoubtedly under the Constitution he has the right to ask advice from whatever source he wishes. In pursuance of that right, he has asked the Secretary of the Treasury to attend all meetings of the Council and later extended the same responsibility to Charles E. Wilson. In the original act, all three of the service secretaries were represented, in addition to the Secretary of Defense. But by the amendment of 1949, the Secretary of Defense was named to act for all the fighting services. The Vice President was also brought in, presumably in some measure to represent the Senate, although the reason given in the legislation is to keep advised the successor to the presidency.

A considerable degree of flexibility has also been followed in inviting other members of the Cabinet or heads of agencies where issues immediately affecting them have been involved. In effect, however, the regular membership has been kept at the level of those Cabinet members and principal advisers to the President named above; though about one half of these are not statutory members of the Council. On the other hand, one of the statutory members, the Chairman of the National

Security Resources Board, at present performs a function of less current importance and magnitude than some of the non-statutory members.

One problem that is important in theory, and which might under certain political conditions become crucial in practice, is whether the Congress ought to give the privilege of participating in the President's policy councils to any official as a matter of right—especially an official over whom the President does not have disciplinary authority. The Vice President, for example, was added to the membership of the Council by the amendments of 1949. With Mr. Barkley and President Truman no difficult issue arises. But in the case of a President and Vice President less politically sympathetic, the President might be so eager to avoid admitting the Vice President to his inner councils that he would make less use of the National Security Council, and perhaps weaken it beyond repair.

Similar to this issue is the question whether, by political pressure, the President may be almost forced to act only on the advice of his subordinates. The MacArthur hearings, which probed into whether the Joint Chiefs of Staff had advised the removal of the General, suggest that the President might sometimes be embarrassed politically by the question whether he had taken a certain action on the advice of his responsible department heads—a question that, as in the case of constitutional monarchy, can be used to restrict an executive's discretion considerably. To escape the limitation, Council recommendations to the President are considered to be to the highest degree privileged.

The Secretary of the Council and the staff are also of considerable importance. Lord Hankey in Britain insisted on keeping his work as Secretary of the Committee of Imperial Defense on a nonpolitical and therefore continuing basis. But he gradually achieved a stature which, on the testimony of the former German Chancellor, Dr. Bruening, involved him directly in many of the most important foreign policy issues and actual negotiations. This has not been true of the Secretary of the National Security Council. Admiral Souers, the first Secretary, appears to have exercised great influence on the President, but his formal function (beyond regular staff preparation of documents) was simply that of bringing to the President the discussions of the Council and the issues still to be resolved where these had not been threshed out or compromised at lower echelons. Mr. James Lay, successor to Admiral Souers, is quite as careful to limit his role to that of a Secretary, rather than that of Chairman.

Both Admiral Souers and Mr. Lay have presided at the meetings of the Senior Staff of the National Security Council. These staff meetings occur at least once a week and sometimes twice or more, depending on the character of the issues involved, and are preparatory for the major Council meetings. The Senior Staff is made up of top-level representatives, usually at the level of Under Secretary or at the least of Assistant Secretary, from the major agencies concerned, including representatives from the Office of Defense Mobilization, from the Mutual Security Administration, and the Psychological Strategy Board. Papers are prepared in response to presidential requests or at the initiation of specific departments or of the staff itself. These are then circulated for comment and, if possible, agreement, first to the Senior Staff and then to the meetings of the Council itself.

Directives may be issued only in the name of the President. But they of course depend for their content in considerable measure on the staff work and interagency consultation which is the main function of the National Security Council.

The present staff practice is to devolve as much as possible on *individual* departments the responsibility for follow-up on Council directives by the President, and also for operating any interdepartmental committee below the level of the National

Security Council itself. There has been an effort to avoid the creation of a sub-committee structure reporting back to the Council.

Undoubtedly this is sound administrative practice. But it does not provide in all cases for the execution of Council directives by sufficiently high-level representatives of the same agencies or by the members of the National Security Council itself. A department or even a bureau which is unsympathetic to a directive may allow it to languish or be "layered" to death at low levels. Nor does this policy of assigning responsibility to agencies rather than to individuals provide in all cases for a follow-up on assigned responsibility for action. The Council may ask for reports through the Secretary, but unless the President himself becomes interested in the matter, there is a marked reluctance to criticize another agency for failure to carry out some policy which may have great joint significance.

The problem of finding a Chairman for the Council to afford it dynamic leadership illustrates its whole nature and difficulties. The President is and must be (as the Prime Minister is in the corresponding body in England) the titular Chairman. On the other hand, except during periods of extreme crisis, it is sometimes argued that the head of government in either case cannot find sufficient time to devote to meetings which occur in the United States on a weekly basis and which in crisis periods have occurred with great regularity in England also. After the outbreak of the Korean hostilities the President did in fact find time to preside at these weekly meetings and has continued the practice. However there is an accepted practice of devolving the chairmanship of the meetings in the rare absence of the President upon the Secretary of State, on the quite logical assumption that the Secretary of State has primary responsibility as well as official seniority in terms of the hierarchy of the Cabinet. There appears to be some disposition in the Defense Department to suggest that in times of grave national crisis or war the chairmanship should perhaps devolve upon the Secretary of Defense, because of the primacy of his task for assuring national survival and the overwhelming shift of attention to this problem. There is also a suggestion that has been made in many quarters (and has found support in our Study Group) that the Special Adviser to the President, who is given the task of coordinating foreign policy with defense policy and foreign aid policy, should normally act as Chairman in the absence of the President.

Good arguments can be made either way. If the chairmanship of the Council carried with it the power of decision or of so influencing recommendations to the President as to affect his decision, it would hardly be likely that the Secretary of State could concede the surrender of the chairmanship to any other Cabinet member or presidential adviser. If, on the other hand, the chairmanship is so used as to develop and explore issues of policy well in advance of their actual formulation and to secure active collaboration among the departments in shaping issues as well as policies for the President, then the chairmanship might readily devolve upon the presidential adviser rather than on the Secretary of State. The Executive Secretary can perform this role and does today initiate many policy questions. In any event, it would seem unwise to devolve the chairmanship on the Secretary of Defense, since even in wartime the conduct of war should be geared into over-all policy on other grounds than the purely military. It is sometimes urged that the Secretary of State would be more free in the advocacy of his own position if he had not the role of Chairman, which might require him to take a neutral position.

It will be seen that much of the validity of either choice will depend upon what the main function of the National Security Council is considered to be. If it becomes an agency that is intended to resolve disputes between the military and the State Department or the Treasury or other economic agencies, including the Bureau of the Budget, no one short of the President can make these decisions and the Council should in all probability have a neutral secretary (or chairman) for their presentation. If, on the other hand, its function is to force and even to anticipate the development of all issues that are implicit in the relations of the economic and fiscal policy of a country with its defense policy and its foreign policy, then a more active leadership for the Council is indicated, and one that does not center in any of the existing departments or agencies.

The working of the Council up to the stage of decision by the President can hardly be one for the resolution of conflicts by authoritative decisions. If there are real conflicts, only the President can choose between alternatives and approve one line of thought or another. The staff work of the Council must then be aimed at recommending as between alternatives or among them. However good staff work can prevent the sharpening of unnecessary conflicts and resolve those less basic. The decisions of the Council itself can get rid of these conflicts, where they are deeply rooted either in clashes of personality or of departmental policies, only by a process that is often deplored: If the pressure for solution by agreement is strong enough, the results may involve a watering down of the language of the papers to a point where it is so vague that all parties feel they can "buy" it. Unless the President devolves a pretty authoritative type of leadership upon the Chairman of the Council who acts for him, or, alternatively, affords to the Council a quite improbable degree of time and active leadership, the Council itself, from its very nature as an interdepartmental committee, is hardly likely to reach authoritative conclusions that will accept one alternative or policy rather than another. It will be more likely either to put a dispute up to the

President for resolution, or to reconcile disputes by the process of accommodation and compromise at the lower level.

In considerable measure the President's method of operating with his intimate White House official family and with political advisers precludes the use of the National Security Council as his top "inner Cabinet." To devolve on a Special Adviser like Harriman the reconciliation of differences also presents very grave problems of setting up an Assistant President at a higher level than either of the two principal Secretaries of his Cabinet, namely, the Secretary of State and the Secretary of Defense.

The same line of analysis applies to the nature of the permanent staff of the National Security Council, depending upon which of the alternatives described above is chosen. The Council may rely on a very small staff of its own and borrow from other agencies for its larger studies, keeping a particularly intimate tie-up with the other top Executive Office coordinating organs, such as the Office of Defense Mobilization, the Mutual Security Administration, and the Bureau of the Budget. This course would be reasonable on the assumption that the Council's function was primarily that of settling disputes and hearing what amounted to appeals. If, on the other hand, it is to become an initiator of policy, shaping the decisive policy papers, it should have a somewhat larger permanent staff of its own, whose careers and promotions would not depend upon the departments concerned; but it could also draw freely for interagency study on other departments for detailed analyses.

There is another important aspect relating to the independence of the Council's staff membership. If the real administrative and disciplinary tie of the staff members is left with the respective departments, they will necessarily tend to function as mouthpieces of their departments, not attempting to think independently and being careful to voice only the opinions given to them by higher-level decisions within their own departments. If they are really freed of departmental ties and placed fully at the disposal of the National Security Council, their status and reactions will be entirely different.

On the other hand, it is something of a dilemma that a too independent status from the departments for staff members of the Council (from a career point of view) often tends to cut off the usefulness of channels which would otherwise remain open. One of the most frequent complaints about the military departments, particularly in their professional sectors, is that they are always less than frank and sometimes positively evasive in communicating either the whole of their plans or their thinking to the National Security Council and the agencies there represented. The military representatives on such a Council's staff have a difficult role under such circumstances. If they intend to continue a military career they tend to be the cautious spokesmen of the fighting services. If they are not primarily intent on this sort of career or are too closely integrated into the permanent staff of the Council, they may find themselves either out of touch with the departments or unfavorably regarded for future promotions.

These difficulties appear to be inherent in the nature of the Council. They can be made less onerous and less a dilemma only to the degree that the President himself uses the Council and comes to rely on it without either attempting to break down the independence of the service agencies in their professional opinions or asking the State Department to water down its own conceptions of foreign policy merely for the sake of getting agreement in matters where military intransigence is especially difficult.

Under quite exceptional circumstances of personal relations between the President and an individual and between that individual and the heads of the Department of State and the

Department of Defense, the devolution of a great degree of responsibility to the President's deputy as Chairman of the Council might produce more active leadership and vitality in its operations. But any high-level integration of policy is bound to present areas where no formula will fit all circumstances and where political leadership and a habit of cooperation are the only answers. It is imperative, however, that our government should not present a spectacle internally in interdepartmental relations at the top levels that resembles the wrangling of representatives of sovereign states and gets action only by accommodation and by something like international diplomacy. Under such circumstances, which appeared to be in some measure characteristic of the period just preceding the outbreak of the North Korean attack, no really effective policy is possible. Action is suspended, and whatever is decided takes on the character of a watered-down compromise, which often lacks the virtues of either clearly pursued alternative.

One possible future for the National Security Council is that it may become, through the preeminence and crucial importance of defense decisions, the top-level sort of "war cabinet" council of the President and the integrating channel for *all* staff work at the White House level. Against this possibility we may set the normal resistance of Cabinet officers and heads of agencies to being "layered" by anyone between them and the President. There may also be some resistance arising from the natural jealousies inherent in the position of the Budget Bureau and perhaps the Council of Economic Advisers, as well as the President's own personal White House staff. Here, as in many other areas, the temperament of a President will determine the solution far more than any lines of organizational analysis. The Study Group has felt unable to do more than suggest here the basic importance of the issues presented and to recommend them as in the highest degree worthy of study, especially within the government, where classified material is available, and by competent students to the degree possible within the limits of security outside the official rings of secrecy.

AD HOC COMMISSIONS

More use should be made by the Executive of the independent *ad hoc* commissions. Mere mention of the Harriman Committee, the Compton Committee, the Acheson-Lilienthal Committee, the Civil Rights Committee, the Finletter Committee, the Hoover Commission, suffice to show the great utility of the representative public committee as a means of clarifying and uniting public opinion on crucial issues.

CONGRESSIONAL RELATIONS

Assuming that the various parts of the executive establishments have been brought into step with each other, the next stage is to persuade Congress to march in the same cadence and direction. Compulsion to this end is repugnant to our present system. Only persuasion will work.

First of all, this requires getting over to the Congress what the direction and cadence are. No one device will suffice. Many are at hand, and the choice of what devices to use must be determined in the light of particular circumstances. These include personal contact between policy-makers and the legislative committees concerned, the widening of legislative awareness through the creation of select committees, the nurturing of informal contacts through social events, informal briefings, and liaison lunches, and, in special instances, the interposition of the President in dealing with the Congress as the ultimate constitutional leader in foreign policy.

Secondly, there is required the development in the Congress of a disposition to go along with an established line. Here the most important thing is to inculcate within the Congress a sense of sharing in the making of policy, for the Congress will be better disposed toward a policy which it has helped to produce than toward one which is the creature of another agency. This requires, to the maximum possible degree, eliciting congressional advice, both in substance and in detail, on legislative proposals. It requires maximum practicable use of members of both Houses in formulating negotiations—provided that their presence generates political strength. It requires—perhaps this most important of all—getting across to Congress and to the public the idea that the Department of State is the defender of American interest and security, not an advocate of foreign interests as ends in themselves.

Finally, the task includes the orientation of the Congress away from using its own powers to counter and neutralize the efforts of the Executive. On the record, Congress is on occasion inclined to create its own line of foreign policy, through enactment of authorizations and appropriations, in such a way as to make them compulsory for the Executive, and, through the use of its investigatory powers, to compel the Executive to follow congressional preconceptions. This, however, is only the obverse of the task of persuading the Congress to go along.

OBSERVATIONS ON THE DEPARTMENT OF STATE

The Department of State from its inception has been judged to be unique among regular departments of the federal government. All matters concerning the foreign relations of this government are properly its concern. It is the focal point for fixing responsibility under the President and within the Executive Branch for the conduct of foreign relations and for matters that affect the relations of the United States with other countries and with international organizations.

Very early experience of the President as well as of the first Secretary of the Treasury (Hamilton) indicated that the relations with Congress of high public officials could not be settled either by legislation or by understandings. The well-known incident in which Washington stalked out of a meeting with the Senate after attempting "consultation" on an early treaty with the Indians, vowing never to return, is a classic case. He did not propose to be treated as the questioning and badgering of the Senate showed that he would be treated if he made personal appearances to ask the advice and consent of that body. Not only Washington's touchy sense of personal dignity but also his feelings for the exalted office which he bore dictated his attitude. It is significant that a President so skillful as Jefferson in having his way with Congress preferred not to repeat the experiment, but to deal with the Senate, so to speak, at arm's length.

Subsequent experience of the Executive, particularly that of the State Department, in trying to bridge the gap almost inevitably created by the separation of powers has run a wide gamut of experimentation. The tradition, however, has been rather strongly fixed that the President shall communicate with the Congress as a whole only in messages of exceptional importance and rarely by direct appearances. The Secretary of State usually approaches Congress directly only through committees dealing with legislative matters which concern the Department. Normally this has meant the Foreign Relations Committee of the Senate and the Foreign Affairs Committee of the House. Only as the Appropriations Committees of the two Houses dealt with his own budget did he appear before them in an *ad hoc* manner until the last decade, when economic policies involving foreign aid became so crucial as to regularize this channel also. The Secretary, by arrangement, may report in unusual and crucial circumstances to the Congress as a whole (as Mr. Hull did after the Moscow Conference). But the experiment initiated by Secretary Acheson of holding an unofficial conference with both Houses for the purpose of answering questions is unique. This device, adopted in May,

1950, has under reasonably favorable conditions, some promise as a new technique, since it makes it possible for the Secretary to meet with the Congress on neutral ground. However, safeguards are necessary to prevent abuse of uncontrolled congressional questions. It is an experiment that should not be too often resorted to and has not in fact been repeated by Mr. Acheson, perhaps because of his own difficulties with a savagely critical segment of the Congress.

Foreign policy has a new importance for the United States which can be measured in part by the more than two thirds of the federal budget that is devoted to foreign economic aid and to military policy—both of which basically condition the realization of foreign policy. It can also be established from a brief look at the increased relevance of foreign policy to total national policy and to all the major aspects of domestic policy.

It is in this new context that the study of the relations of the Department of State in particular, and of the Executive Branch as a whole, to Congress must be set if any realistic appraisal of the modern problem is to be made. New precedents have emerged with new responsibilities. A much more flexible opportunity for experiment obviously exists in the light of new problems and public attitudes.

The task of getting the ear of Congress and persuading that body to favorable action is made even harder by the circumstance that no strong lobbying groups of vitally concerned citizens are at hand to ease the way for foreign policy legislation. The State Department, which vouches for such legislation, is almost inevitably thrust into the role of claimant for foreign interests rather than for particular domestic interests. Moreover, the Department operates abroad; it has small opportunity to establish its support in the domestic grass roots. Thus the separation of powers, enjoined by the Constitution and made particularly broad as to foreign policy, is further widened by the simple political facts of life.

We feel that the basic error of the State Department is its wholly unwarranted disposition to limit narrowly the area of its interests, especially where there is a question of possible conflict with the Department of Defense. This assertion may seem surprising to those who know how often and how energetically, in recent years, the Department of State has tangled with the military powers. The point is that these largely private struggles are, at least in part, the result of a basic and preliminary surrender of authority. The Department of State seems to share, and not to oppose, the national feeling that force and policy are somewhat distinct; and by seeming to share this feeling, it encourages the persistence of this myth, thus weakening its control of policy.

According to this view (stated a little sweepingly, it may be), every time the State Department acts as if the Defense Department were somehow a separate source of wisdom, able to furnish counsel from a special and at least coequal eminence, every time a Secretary of State dismisses a policy-connected military problem as a matter for soldiers, every time the men of force are deferred to by the men of policy, the chance for a united and effective national foreign policy is decreased. Every such action tends to recognize and to perpetuate a separation between military and political matters. And they cannot be separated. This is the first point. And a second one follows at once. If a separation is recognized, a supremacy cannot be asserted; thus in this event, the attitude of the Department would clearly debar it from a successful attempt to take charge of American foreign policy.

Our discussion of the preceding considerations produced agreement on the need for integration so that a single policy should emerge. But we were not equally agreed that the State Department could always adequately assess the military factors or that a resolution short of the President, with the advice of the National Security Council, either should or could be forced.

However, on any view, it appears that the Department of State is a major and in part a voluntary contributor to its own ineffectiveness. Granted that its separation from problems of force is not entirely of its own making, there is the public disposition to seek and to follow a direct military opinion, so conspicuous in the case of the Congress; and the jealously guarded self-sufficiency of military leaders, so conspicuous in the history of the Joint Chiefs of Staff. Finally, we must recognize that as a practical matter most workaday military affairs must be decided and controlled by military men, not policy-makers; their connection to policy is vital, but even when it is recognized and honored, the work itself remains military. All these factors operate to limit the influence of the State Department, especially if that influence is conceived as a direct control over field soldiers. Nevertheless, we feel justified in pointing to what we regard as a neglect of obligation on the part of the leaders of the State Department.

SUGGESTED REFORMS FOR THE DEPARTMENT OF STATE

Our basic conclusion on the Department of State is that by the nature of its assignment it must assert and sustain a real primacy among the departments of government in shaping our foreign policy, and that the most obvious difficulty in this responsibility lies in its own insufficient self-assertion with respect to the military.

INTERNAL

The Department should take over all foreign operations (as distinct from *policies*) that are not strictly military in character, and there should be appointed a Secretary for Foreign Operations who would be a sort of general manager for the Department for all overseas operations. This post should be junior to the Secretary for Foreign Policy, both of whom would be responsible to a new and more elevated Secretary of State who would hold a higher position on an organization chart, like that of the Secretary of Defense. The Secretary of State would thus have under him one Secretary not of Cabinet rank for policy and one Secretary not of Cabinet rank for operations, just as the Secretary of Defense has under him non-Cabinet Secretaries for Air, Army, and Navy.

More emphasis should be put on the over-all economic policy aspects of foreign policy, and this area of the Department of State should be strengthened. The swing toward regional assignment of responsibility, even though coupled with a Policy Planning Staff, may have gone too far.

It may be possible to broaden the Department's "reserve officers corps" with refresher briefings for its members and to start something like the Navy League, under well-chosen auspices, for support before the public. The aid of certain foundations might appropriately be sought to this end, but the entire matter has pitfalls so serious as to deserve most careful weighing.

VIS-A-VIS THE MILITARY

The State Department, to summarize our opinion, ought not to take too limited a view of its responsibilities. Wherever a policy problem arises—even if on the surface it is mainly a military matter—the State Department should have a voice, and, under the President, it should have a leading voice. The present ineffectiveness of the Department in this area arises, at least in part, from default of the role of defender of the national interest.

Emphasis has been put upon the increased need for training military officials in relevant areas that will affect their future operations in relation to civilian policy. Equally, an emphasis ought to be laid and, in some measure is being laid, on the training of State Department and other government officials whose duties require a correct assessment of military capacities and operations, as well as direct acquaintance with personnel and with types of military thinking and behavior. Reference has been made to the assignment of State Department officials to the war colleges, which has this reciprocal benefit. This practice should be increased within the limits of available personnel. Greater emphasis on military history and the organization of wartime mobilization, and on the handling of strategic-materials problems and the utilization of national power to this end, seems to be essential in the training of the officials of the State Department, Foreign Service, and officers of the Economic Cooperation Administration and other civilian agencies dealing with foreign relations

VIS-À-VIS CONGRESS

The President and the Secretary of State in approaching Congress should appear, in so far as this role is compatible with the true education of opinion, as the defenders of national interests and protectors of American security, rather than as advocate for the foreigner against domestic critics.

The Administration's foreign policy program should be presented so far as possible in "general package bills," to avoid unnecessary clutterings of the congressional calendar and to obtain a coherent legislative program. Better preparation in advance for legislative proposals would help to avoid irritation in Congress which results from being continuously confronted with piecemeal and crisis legislation.

The Secretary of State might, on selected occasions, and at his initiative, or at the very least with his consent, make personal appearances before both Houses and, under carefully prepared conditions, answer questions. Control of the question period should be arranged in some measure by having a series of questions submitted in writing and beforehand, to permit the Secretary time for preparation. Skillfully handled, this could be an excellent device for presenting the Department's views effectively.*

Greater effort should be made by the Department to furnish relevant material to specific Congressmen and to make available in advance to all members of Congress information now regularly made available to newspaper commentators and lecturers. Although fixed rules cannot govern this matter, a sound policy would be to furnish Congress with as much information as it needs for its decisions, in spite of the abuses and leaks which this induces. Instances like the "leak" on the number of now ready "B-36's" discourage this willingness—for a time at least. But they emphasize the need for more congressional responsibility, and this can come only with experience and from a tradition which can only grow with sharing the need for protecting really vital "security secrets."

The Assistant Secretary for liaison with Congress should work out arrangements for liaison meetings with the same care that is taken in foreign missions to arrange a proper setting for the most informal aspects of negotiations.

The most effective liaison with the Congress can be achieved on an informal rather than a formal basis, and as such it is worth great care and attention, however wearying and time-consuming.

An effort should be made to broaden the rather routine meetings at Prospect House by inviting groups from interested committees of the House of Representatives and by dinner meetings with selected groups of Senators

---

* If a constitutional amendment embodying voting seats for members of the Executive Branch were adopted, of course the matter might be settled. But at present, appearance on demand before each House of Congress for questions probably would raise more problems than it would solve.

The Department should endeavor to broaden the direct liaison with committees and the normal efforts to get advice from key congressional figures, not limited to the key committees.

Some of the difficulties of drafting bills might be shared with these congressional leaders. "Sheer attitude" in this respect on the part of the Department is of tremendous importance. A Congressman consulted as a partner, *in advance,* is a Congressman mollified, if not completely won over

It is important to recognize that the new role of the Department demands a new accountability from the Department. Congressional relations can be improved by recognizing that diplomacy, even more than charity, begins at home. The legitimate role that Congress is entitled to play on an informed basis is a first article of faith for an effective foreign policy. Topside recognition of this fact, a thorough briefing of subordinates, and a determined follow-through by the Department's high command are essential in order to change traditional attitudes.

The Department should select certain members of the Congress to "carry the ball" for the Administration, through speeches and articles, on an item-by-item basis (not just on a bill-by-bill basis) on important issues of bipartisan policy.

Great progress has been made by the Department in the recognition of this necessity and in an improvement of techniques. There is evidence that the Department has put real study into the selection of appropriate individuals in Congress for both informal consultation and for sponsoring on the Hill important measures of the Department. It is not always the State Department itself which can best achieve these informal contacts. But it should always be the Department's effort to see that they are arranged by those within the Administration, or outside it, who can explain and clarify and, at need, defend the Department's views effectively.

VIS-À-VIS THE PUBLIC

The Department is always under attack for using its information media to advance a partisan policy. Actually, the program of the Department must be, under any conditions, the resultant of a national policy. Whoever wins the elections must speak for the nation. Democracy must not, in the interest of partisanship, cripple the spokesmen of the nation—the President and his Secretary of State—from fear. Restraints through political timidity on the methods of educating the public to the issues involved result in a weak policy and an uninformed and apathetic public. This is one of the most important instances in which an increase in executive discretion must go hand in hand with a better and a bolder use of the necessary powers. Whoever is charged with the administration of our government must be able both to speak for our nation and make the nation understand its case. The Secretary of State generally gains politically from a boldness in taking the offensive politically.

The Department must have strong political backing for its program through wide public support, especially when the Secretary is not himself a major political figure. This means increasing emphasis on public relations as well as on congressional relations.

Every effort should be made to build up strong public opinion and to keep in touch with opinion as far as possible through contacts at the "grass roots."

Private organizations, such as citizens' committees with support in farm and labor circles, should be found to remedy the lack of pressure groups interested in supporting the Department. Utilization of such bodies of leading citizens as the Committee to Defend America by Aiding the Allies is entirely compatible with the nature of the democratic process.

More speeches by trained officials, particularly returning Foreign Service officers, along with the fullest possible ex-

ploitation of speech-making consultants and volunteer citizens'
committees, are needed. Radio and television time and maga-
zine articles are also helpful when intelligently used.

In sum there should be a far more effective and systematic
attempt to explain the moral and historical necessities behind
our foreign policy to the people who must ultimately support it.
This is not a partisan performance but a public duty. Of course
the avenues for criticism must be left open to all but controlled
enemy agents.

OBSERVATIONS ON THE DEPARTMENT OF DEFENSE

The great single overriding deficiency in the Executive Branch
is that there is a wholly insufficient connection between the
policy-makers and the soldiers. This is not, of course, a new
complaint. Students have emphasized the point for years, and
leading members of successive Cabinets have tried to improve
relationships. The most notable recent effort is the National
Security Council which has already had a brief analysis. There
can be no doubt that this presidential staff agency has served
to bring together men of State and Defense at reasonably high
levels, providing senior consideration of common problems.
There is much additional evidence of a reaching out from both
departments toward each other—the National War College, the
interchange of staff personnel, the slow decline of the habit of
separate and untainted thought in the Joint Chiefs of Staff
and at the policy levels of the State Department. All of those
are welcome signs that policy and strategy are nowadays at
least aware of one another. Nevertheless there are two important problems in connection with the Joint Chiefs of Staff:
how to make that body more political minded and less military
minded; and, on the other hand, how to have the civilian
agencies learn to imitate its useful techniques.

By the standards of the argument, the surface has hardly

been scratched. Whereas *all* problems relating to the use of force should be considered as part of the general pattern of policy, the present set-up at its best can hardly do more than insure that policy and armed forces do not directly conflict. The coordination so far achieved is essentially negative and fragmentary. There is a loose coalition between the strategists and the men of policy, but there is no unification. Secretary Marshall, in testifying before the "Russell" Committee on the MacArthur dismissal, gave evidence of an appreciation of this weakness and indicated his efforts to provide a closer integration of military with foreign policy at all levels of the Department of Defense with the Department of State.

SUGGESTED REFORMS IN THE DEPARTMENT OF DEFENSE

If policy and force are to be integrated effectively, the power and prestige of the civilian Secretaries of the armed forces—particularly the standing and powers of the Secretary of Defense—must be widely extended. In essence, the Secretary of Defense and his associates must become the effective agents of the President in all that relates to the armed forces. This view, which has been gaining in strength since World War II, involves a considerable and still incomplete change from the ordinary position of the ordinary service secretary in the years before 1945. On the effectiveness of the Secretary of Defense rests much of the prospects for real civilian control.

Between the Commander in Chief and the Joint Chiefs of Staff, where is the place for the civilian Secretary? It is a tough question, and it has been answered in two contradictory ways, both of them partly embodied in the National Security Act of 1947, as amended. On the one hand, the wartime Joint Chiefs and military men generally held that the key to the effectiveness of their organization was its direct access to the President. On the other hand, there was a large group of students who hoped to achieve a new level of military effectiveness by creating a new Secretary of Defense with great central powers. This group, which grew in numbers and influence as weaknesses of the 1947 Act were revealed, naturally hoped to see the Joint Chiefs brought directly under the Secretary of Defense. The amendments of 1949 sidestep the issue; the Joint Chiefs report to both the Secretary and the President. Clearly it is a matter of presidential discretion whether it becomes normal for them to regard the Secretary as boss. At the very least, it is now possible. The present contention is that the Secretary of Defense cannot do his job unless this control is recognized, enforced, and made customary.

In our view the correct conception of the task of the Secretary of Defense is that he is the Deputy Commander in Chief, exercising from day to day the full authority of the President in military matters.

It is important to emphasize the special policy-making function of the Secretary of Defense. In the end, this job is the real key to both the unity of the Executive Branch and the primacy of policy. Only when the Secretary of Defense is himself a man of policy, and an effective deputy to the President, will it be possible for the counsels of the *State* Department to receive their due weight. A line of decision and counsel which goes from the Secretary of State to the Secretary of Defense to the Joint Chiefs of Staff is proper and practicable; a direct line to the Joint Chiefs from the Department of State cannot do the job. And for big matters, the basic issues, all hands must turn to the President. These three men, the President, the Secretary of State, and the Secretary of Defense, are necessarily a team, and none of them can do his job without the others. Nor is this to deny in any way the observation made earlier that the President's personal responsibility for the conduct of foreign policy must be strengthened in response to the times.

The Secretary of Defense is quite clearly a key figure in the arch that this relationship establishes for the control and even for the conduct of basic aspects of foreign policy and operations. His span of control has been broadened to include much more than the already widespread problems of military assistance and the allocation of arms and military aid on a global basis. Even under this direct military responsibility he has outposts under his control that are exposed to perpetual risks of precipitating incidents, of having to prevent the development of pressures that could be worse than incidents. He still has occupational powers and responsibility in areas like Korea and some remaining problems in Japan and in Germany, as well as responsibility for bases for the Air Force and for the Navy and supporting detachments in many other areas in foreign lands.

But in addition to this direct military responsibility which involves foreign policy in some of its most important operational phases, the Secretary of Defense has an extended span of control through the Scientific Research and Development area of his office. A great part of the most important developments in warfare and in the power equation are wrapped up in this office. The research and the types of problems which are studied by the Rand Corporation, for example, cover many aspects of psychological warfare and intelligence analysis at a high level. These projects may carry important consequences in their application to foreign policy. The intelligence services of the military forces themselves, and the participation of the Defense Department in the control of the Central Intelligence Agency, present an enormous range of responsibility and control involving, in a period of mixed cold and hot war, paramilitary features of the greatest possible consequence to the conduct of foreign policy.

The equipment of the Secretary of Defense to handle this span of control through his civilian staff is of crucial importance. It is no accident and it is indeed of the greatest benefit that there has been a considerable interchange of ability by the Secretaries of Defense and the Secretaries of State, beginning with Secretary Stimson, proceeding through Secretary Marshall, and now with Secretary Lovett a continuation of the same type of interchangeable experience. Conceivably the experience of the Secretary of Defense is also an admirable preparation for a change in the other direction, namely, from Defense to State.

The Munitions Board, too, offers a great range for extension of the Secretary of Defense's responsibility and control of matters vitally affecting foreign policy. The Munitions Board not only enters the entire context of domestic mobilization in the most direct way in contract authority and the direction of procurement; it is involved also in problems of joint production —as, for example, with Canada—and in the use of facilities in Japan, Germany, and elsewhere. Its stockpile objectives and its decisions as to the nature and importance of strategic and critical materials push the limits of the economic system of the United States to the ends of the earth. In its civilian component it must necessarily develop thinking that is typical of the problems we have steadily incurred in recognizing the place of military security in the broader context of political strength and the moral posture of the United States.

If the Secretary of Defense is to have the basic powers of a Deputy Commander in Chief, it is obviously important that he be able to maintain a real, and not a fictitious, control over his Department. For this purpose, the first and foremost requirement is participation by the Secretary in the presidential exercise of the power of appointment. The President should give the Secretary of Defense great influence in the selection of the Chiefs of Staff. The second basic need of the Secretary is a staff of its own. In this respect the National Security Act of 1949 improves upon that of 1947, but it is by no means lavish. It is of the first importance that the Secretary of Defense be free to employ, as his own men, substantial numbers of the senior staff, in and out of uniform. The caliber and expertness of this staff, plus its loyalty to the office of the Secretary, will condition the success of any civilian control over the military. The need for such personnel is particularly great in these early, formative years of the tradition of the Defense Department when it is so exceedingly important to bring the Joint Chiefs of Staff into lasting and flexible subordination to the civilian executive.

Yet it is no part of the purpose of these suggestions to invade the legitimate functions of the Joint Chiefs or of any other military unit. The powers here urged for the Defense Secretary are powers that have always belonged to the President; we are talking not so much about a "Super-Secretary" as about a sub-Commander in Chief. It is not the military job, but the President's job—the policy job—that has been imperfectly done in the past.

We give this point particular emphasis because we do not share the frequently expressed suspicion of "the military mind." If in recent years military men have occasionally played a somewhat outsize role in policy-making, the cause is to be found more in the timidity and indecision of civilians than in any grasping "militarism." In general, military men have shown rather more sense in the field of policy than policy-makers have shown in the field of force. Certainly an occasional officer persistently trespasses into policy, and probably nearly every officer trespasses a little, here and there. It would be remarkable if it were not so. Still the remedy is always at hand for the civilian authority with courage. It is not our military men who must be weakened; it is our makers of policy who must gain strength. We are not attacking the "military mind." We are instead, trying to make a case for the "political mind" on the premise that this is, in the end, the age of the political man. This political man is no enemy of force; he must rather be its understanding student and in some degree its skilled employer, even if his skills can keep his nation from an all-out war. This is the political man who must have control, and our argument drives only to this central point; that this control, constitutionally and correctly, belongs to the elected President, his Secretary of State, and his Secretary (who is his deputy) for Defense. There is nothing to prove that a soldier cannot have a great political mind; there is much present evidence to the contrary. But there really is no need to argue that the soldier, *as soldier,* must not make the policy decisions. They are the province of political leaders.

What improvements can be expected if the State Department, the Defense Department, and the Presidency are strengthened along the lines here urged? Our answer is that the proposed changes would strengthen the framing of policy, unify its operation, and permit a far higher degree of positive and purposeful action.

IV

THE ROLE OF THE LEGISLATURE
IN THE FORMULATION AND CONTROL
OF FOREIGN POLICY

OBSERVATIONS ON THE LEGISLATURE

THE CONGRESS has a much larger role in foreign affairs than it once did because of the need for heavy appropriations for foreign economic and military aid, as well as for the maintenance of an expensive domestic military establishment. Moreover, Congress supervises the administration of the Executive Branch in great detail. Indeed, Congress has many more powers than it actually exercises; but, be it noted, the *right* to exercise these powers does not make their exercise expedient. As a matter of fact, the United States is the only English-speaking nation which permits the legislative body to determine tenure and service of employees of the government; to amend the budget; to organize below the top levels of executive departments; to control by statute the conditions and status of the civil and military services; to deal directly with all levels of the administrative hierarchy on questions of policy and administration. In practice, if the legislature wants to change a policy, its inclination is to do so administratively, either by saying that such and such a person must go, or else that such and such a function must be reorganized. Direct election of the Senate, open committee hearings, and a more intimate working relation with the press, the radio, and organized pressure groups have altered Congress's relation to the party organizations, to the Executive, and to the public. Nevertheless, Congressmen generally remain spokesmen for local rather than national interests, and they are not required by their position to assume responsibility for executing the policies they legislate. They get elected in local constituencies, often on the basis of local politics, not at large or by being chosen "to stand" for the party and its program.

Party discipline within the Congress has weakened during the past half century. This is the result of a variety of causes— among them the popular election of Senators, the fact that most committee hearings have been opened to public testimony, the development of "canned broadcasts," and the use of the franking privilege to popularize the independent rewards of the Congressmen. Whatever the cause, there is hardly any other form to supplement party discipline. Committees are virtually independent political forces, and the chairmen and members hold their positions by seniority, not by their willingness to support the policies of their respective parties. This is, if not the greatest, at least one of the principal elements of irresponsibility in the American constitutional system. And, significantly enough, it depends not on any clause in the Constitution, but merely on tradition and on the rules of each House. Although the bugaboo of Executive Caesarism is often raised, there really is not much danger that the Congress will yield its powers to the Executive except in time of extreme national peril and such confusion as to render democratic procedures impotent. Otherwise it will always be in the interest of members of the Congress to proclaim their independence and their constitutional rights. There is at present a much greater danger that Congress will yield its powers to congressional committees. As long as each member has his share of committee influence, he will not raise a voice in objection to this really sinister shift of authority from the whole to the separate parts.

One group of political scientists in the academic profession is quite content with the pressure type of congressional organization which the American system accommodates thus uniquely. Indeed, this school of thought considers "flexibility" to be the genius of the American people, on the theory that the pressures really give the system its dynamic. Some even argue that the party system as it operates in the national legislature is ideally suited to blurring issues so that no sharp division in the country can tear the nation apart. On the other hand, there are political scientists who argue that if a programmed policy for action is necessary, as it always is where national security is involved, the nation cannot afford the waste involved in blurring issues. This group points to tariff bills, for example, or merchant marine legislation, and says that if such as these are the result of pressures, then the dynamic is wrong and the system should be strengthened in order to get true "programmatic responsibility" in the legislature.

Perhaps a word of explanation of the concept of "programmatic responsibility" is in order since this is the key to the major over-all reform needed in the formation and control of foreign policy in the United States. Its particular focus in the discussion of the legislature does not preclude its necessary application to the Executive, to the party system, and to the methods by which the electorate brings its wishes to bear upon the system as a whole.

Theories of democracy have always stressed the competence of the public to act in one of three ways: (1) Directly, either by popular assembly or by initiative or referendum. This method is inapplicable as to any popular assembly beyond the town meeting, and as to the initiative and referendum for any but the most limited type of broad (and not urgent or deadline) public policy. It is therefore peculiarly unsuited to foreign policy issues. (2) Representation in accordance with the varieties of public attitudes, which in an extreme form may be found in J. S. Mills's emphasis on proportional representation in *Representative Government*. Variations on this theme are to be found in forms of functional representation—"the butcher, the baker and the candlestick maker"; in the French system of *blocs;* and on a non-official basis in the "interest-group" type of pressure on legislatures found especially in the United States. All of these methods have the common disadvantage of producing a government that cannot "govern"—that is, one that cannot operate on the basis of a coherent program. (3) A form of representation that selects representatives on a broad basis of party responsibility, rather than on merely local issues, or a special interest representation, or narrow divisions of any sort. This requires compromising many lesser disagreements in order to achieve the kind of party government somewhat idealized by Edmund Burke but more realistically treated by Walter Bagehot. Such a government has a mandate to accomplish a program. Its responsibilty may therefore be called "programmatic."

In no field is "programmatic responsibility" more important than in foreign policy.

The question therefore is whether the form of government which we now have in the United States adequately promotes "programmatic responsibility" for foreign policy and whether public opinion finds effective channels to this end. It is our view that achievement of "programmatic responsibility" in the American system grows more and more difficult wtih the passage of time. However it is not possible to say with finality whether the Executive's problem of persuading the Congress is greater than the Congressmen's problem of persuading constituents to reelect them for office. Some estimate of this balance is necessary in order to place the responsibility for a new initiative in obtaining "programmatic responsibility" for the government as a whole.

Now from the general to the specific: It is clear that the Constitution gives to Congress the power to make the rules governing the armed forces; to provide the men and the money they need; and, by logical extension, to be informed of what they do and why. Obviously Congress cannot be ignored in the framing of foreign or even of military policy; if it chooses, it can exert a controlling influence.

It is of course clearly a necessity in any constitutional system that the legislative branch should have the power to control the armed services. This is not to say that it is always desirable for this power to be asserted; our general argument is rather that it must ordinarily be used sparingly, and that in times of danger the Legislature (as its own members will usually recognize) must accept a distinctly secondary role. Yet the right to assert a firm control is central. The clear-cut constitutional rights of the Congress in the field of armed forces are a vital check in the system of checks and balances. As long as it retains the *right* to intervene, Congress is safe in accepting as normal the fact that the basic formulation of military plans and programs is a task for the Executive Branch.

It seems to us that the Congress in the main is doing what it ought to do in the field of armed force, including the following: reserving final and plenary authority only for crisis situations; exercising its right and duty to pass, regularly, on the order of magnitude of military effort; recognizing that basic planning responsibilities and technical decisions must be left to the Executive Branch; undertaking a "watch-dog" function, including full rights of information.

There is, however, one major qualification—one area in which the customs and practices of the Congress are seriously out of line. The attitude of Congress denies that the problem of armed force in all its aspects is essentially only a *part* of the problem of policy. Congressmen and Senators constantly encourage the discussion of military problems in purely military terms, and constantly prefer the man in uniform to the man in mufti as a source of information and advice. The "why" is in dispute. It deserves deep attention.

SUGGESTED REFORMS FOR THE LEGISLATURE

There should be continued improvement in the following trends which have been developing over the last half century:

More informal consultation between the Executive Branch and congressional leaders, as in the President's regular meetings with the "Big Four," that is, the political leadership of each House.

The President should prepare and submit to the Congress and the people a more comprehensive program for consideration as a whole. The budget is a step in this direction; it could be made into a system of comprehensive responsibility if the Joint Committee on Internal Revenue Taxation were willing to require the Executive to submit a revenue program, as it now submits an expenditure program. The Economic Report is another such step; it could lead to much more coordination if the Congress were willing to give the Joint Committee on the Economic Report the right to coordinate legislative committees.

A foreign policy legislative program ought to exist, at least in the main outlines, for each session of Congress. No such program can be rigid in the face of the rapidly changing circumstances and crises of the contemporary world. It should be recognized also on the part of Congress that the duty of Congress in legislative authorization is to establish broad policies rather than to institute detailed scrutiny of administrative performance in the legislative stage. There is sometimes a necessary protective tendency on the part of a harried Executive to overestimate, and therefore to defeat the aims of congressional scrutiny. It is however admittedly healthy for the Executive Department to have to organize its case for congressional presentation.

A half century ago there was no separate appropriations committee; eight specialized committees divided up the estimates for consideration and acknowledged no relationship among them. When Congress as a whole was persuaded that finance was an important consideration that cut across all aspects of policy and legislation, it set up a separate Appropriations Committee and decided that after a legislative committee handled a statute setting a policy, the money had to be provided through the Appropriations Committee. Perhaps we are at this stage now with respect to foreign policy. Perhaps other committees will have to submit to some review—through some procedure—by either a central policy committee, or by the foreign relations or the foreign affairs committee in each House at a higher level of political authority than is now the case.

Moreover, the appropriations committee system was not effective without a corresponding arrangement at the executive end, so the Congress provided by law that it would not act on estimates without getting presidential recommendation.

Next, as it discovered that reorganization was needed for economy, it provided that the President could submit a Reorganization Plan, and that neither House could amend it, or filibuster on it. Congress decided that on this issue it would have to say yes or no, with no quibbling or stalling, by a record vote.

In principle, these steps have tremendous potentialities, leading to much greater legislative integration and much greater cooperation with the Executive.

Alternatively, of course, one could move toward the greater

disciplinary party responsibility of the British system in order to insure a program.

The duties of Congress with respect to the Armed Forces should strengthen those traditionally asserted, in line with those increasingly practiced today, as just previously noted.

The constitutional powers of the Congress go further than those cited above, but cannot be usefully exercised in full. The Congress in fact does a respectable job now on the above pattern, and this is in the main what it should be doing. A major failing in emphasis on the part of the Congress is its tendency to "give up" on the problem of forcing a considered application of the budget to a really balanced concept of the uses of the armed forces in accordance with a basic strategy. This is perhaps a measure of poor civilian leadership and weakness in the office of the Secretary of Defense, but pressure by Congress could strengthen rather than weaken the Secretary.

The Congress currently gives a special weight to military men and military considerations. In principle, this special weight is undesirable even when the military men are wise and good, in so far as it treats the uniform as a source of some miraculous and special oracular wisdom. It is undesirable that military and political considerations should be separated, and equally undesirable that they should be so connected that military considerations come first. This is a major criticism that results from a measurement of present congressional practice against the theoretical standards of this inquiry. Yet even this complaint is more apparent than real, for the remedy in this case is more in the Executive than in the Legislative Branch. Until the Executive Branch organizes its control of its military men and weights power politics adequately, it is too much to expect the Congress to rely on civilian leadership alone.

Cooperation is a two-way street. In the first place, Congress must have a serious interest in foreign policy. In the second place, influential Congressmen who want to share in the formulation of policy must not expect to take important stands themselves on foreign policy issues without going through a process of reciprocal prior consultation with the Executive. In the third place, Congress must provide really good staffs for their committees; real opportunities for fruitful collaboration may exist on the staff level between congressional committees and executive departments.

When one is confronted with proposals for improving the machinery for dealing with foreign policy and particularly for strengthening Congress's ability to cope with the problems involved in coordinating legislative attitude, there is sometimes an understandable tendency to despair. Most of the usual pat suggestions that are made, such as having joint hearings between the two committees principally dealing with foreign affairs in the House and Senate, show a complete lack of realistic grasp of the nature of our bicameral system. No Senate Committee is ever going to agree to submerge its own membership in the large joint committee that would result. It is entirely impracticable to work out rules for an equal division of time in questions to witnesses as between the House members and the Senate members as sub-groups in such joint hearings. Legislative formulation of a single bill would be impossible.

Again, since it is deeply engrained in the customary practice of Congress—though the seniority principle is bad and sometimes tragic—it is politically very deeply rooted. Substitutes for its automatic working could only be introduced along with other reforms which would greatly strengthen the disciplinary hold of the party leaders in Congress.

There is a genuine need for stronger central policy committee staffs for both parties in both Houses, with greater emphasis on tie-in by the policy staffs to the staffs of legislative committees.

But to achieve this reform it is necessary to convince the political leadership that systematic control of policy is superior to the present flexibility of consulting when, as, and if, the need arises. Legislative leaders are almost as overburdened as executive leaders. Furthermore, there is so little party discipline and so great a need for bipartisanship on foreign policy issues that there may be some real wisdom in not systematizing these matters by staffing the Speaker of the House or the policy committees for more effective central study of programs—inevitably a party staff, and since so chosen, so treated. To change the present practice would, as in other matters, require many other changes to fit the reform.

No doubt the committees themselves can and should continue to improve the subcommittee structure, in order to expedite bills of smaller importance and to increase the activity and prestige of individual members. The staffing of all the committees of Congress presents great difficulty in terms of tenure. But continuity for capable staff members is at least as important in the area of foreign affairs as in appropriations or any of the other committees which have achieved something of this character. Building up the Legislative Reference Service would extend greatly the efficiency of the committee staffs and would in some measure supply a flexible central staff for Congress, which should be particularly strengthened in the area of defense and foreign policy. But the use of this existing staff continually rouses staff jealousies among the legislative committees. A good man tends to be taken over by the committees, either permanently or, on what amounts to the same thing, on "loan."

Committee chairmen might also be expected to encourage, more than at present, staff responsibility for following the discussion and progress of bills in committees, other than Foreign Affairs and Foreign Relations, which have a direct bearing on foreign policy. A preoccupied chairman is sometimes confronted with what amounts to a *fait accompli* in the action of another committee of which he has had very little warning. Broadening the State Department's liaison with other committees to assist in this task would be most useful, since the Department *must* be on the lookout for such issues, and would tend to alert the committees with primary responsibility for foreign policy.

The peculiar primacy of the Appropriations Committees in their effect on foreign policy needs to be mitigated by the right of members of the Foreign Affairs, Foreign Relations, and Armed Services Committees to be consulted when matters affecting them are under consideration by the Appropriations Committees. The Senate has worked out a partial approach to this, but the practice is completely absent in the House.

There should certainly be an extension of the properly qualified special (or select) study committees under appropriate leadership and with full cooperation by the executive departments. The excellent work done, for example, by House Special Committees, such as the Colmer and Herter committees, clearly broadens the receptivity of the legislative body for important aspects of foreign policy. Sneers at "junketing" require modification in the light of the reports and influence of such committees and the strenuous work and study engaged in by their members and staffs. The important point is to control the character of these committees and make them representative, in a useful way, of the sense of the *whole* House or of the Senate. Informal trips by members of different committees have their usefulness, but they are not productive of systematic results unless regularized. The House practice of inviting members of other important committees to participate in hearings is of some use, but of little broad practical effect.

The Senate's practice of holding joint sessions of the committees on Foreign Relations and Armed Services on such matters as the MacArthur dismissal and the Mutual Security Assistance program suggests similar procedure in the House; though the difficulties of increasing the size of House committees for purposes of hearings is acknowledged.

One must admit, finally, that legislative committees will continue to carry the burden of responsibility for framing programs into law; and that Congress, so long as it lacks party discipline, will have to rely upon various stages and hurdles, like the Rules Committee and the Appropriations Committees, for screening and for control. These devices are largely negative in their effects. Congress must ultimately rely also upon its leadership on the floor to protect a program formulated by the committee with legislative authority while it is running the gantlet of amendments. Without more sweeping and basic reforms involving methods of election, it is difficult to see how Congress is going to change its nature.

Mid-term elections should be abolished, even though this requires a constitutional amendment. They are not a healthy imperative for the country as a whole nor for the conduct of foreign policy. That much structural change in the government seems clearly indicated.

PART TWO

THE ULTIMATE CONTROL
IN A DEMOCRACY

V

PUBLIC OPINION AND THE
ELECTORAL PROCESS

T HERE ARE those who see the real question of organized
democratic society only in terms of the "squeal level" and
the mechanics for altering it. That is a scurrilous view of
democracy, certainly of constitutional democracy.

The role of public opinion and its competence to deal with
foreign policy has always been one of the most broadly dis-
puted and basic issues. Ultimately all political mechanisms
depend upon the fundamental conception of the nature of
public opinion, its limits, and how it can be expected to function through representative machinery. This, as we have noted,
depends in turn on the broad concepts of human nature and
the political ability of particular nations.

Throughout a great deal of history the basic defense of the
elitist position has been that the public is incapable of understanding the issues on which its own survival depends and that
it must rely upon "guardians" (Plato) or the Grand Inquisitor
of Dostoevski's *Brothers Karamazov* to estimate the necessary
sacrifices and secure their enforcement. In the classic exposition of liberalism by John Locke, the "federative power"
(which dealt with foreign affairs) was to be separate from the
ordinary workings of legislative and executive powers in order
to insure its independent functioning with broad discretion
and freedom from really responsible public control. Locke

anticipated even much later British practice of the Foreign Office because of the prime need for secrecy, prestige, and the nation's survival. In a time like our own, theorists who are entirely sympathetic with the general necessity for constitutional democracy (for example, Professor Carl J. Friedrich) have tended to rule out of the competence of the common man the basic issues of foreign policy, either as to their formulation or their control. But, pushed to any extreme length, such a view merely writes off the possibilities of democratic survival, since foreign policy determines so much of all the rest of a nation's policy.

It has been our general underlying theory of democracy that, in order to survive, democracies must expand and co-operate with other like-minded constitutional systems in order to establish a world where constitutional processes might be gradually extended into the international sphere. Extreme exponents of democracy have gone so far as to suggest that devices like the Ludlow Referendum—which would not have permitted declaration of war without direct popular sanction—would prevent the outbreak of war. Other extremists have talked (as in World War I) as if making the world safe for democracy means democratizing all humanity—if need be, by a sort of holy war or crusade. These are extreme views. But a "necessary minimum" theory would insist on preserving a core of strength founded on mature constitutional systems adequate to deter totalitarian expansion.

As between these extremes there is recognition that public opinion in a healthy democracy (and that is only possible at a very mature stage of modern civilization) can only operate on the broad principles of policy and on the basic directions in which the state should move. It obviously cannot enforce the same measures everywhere except by a crusading war to make the world democratic, instead of merely safe for democracy. But it must attempt, by all the means at its disposal, to create conditions that will limit the effectiveness of resort to force in a world where surprise attacks carry such chances of success. A *sine qua non* of this effort is to secure an overwhelming alignment of power on the side of like-minded states with a respect for constitutional processes. Unless, indeed, there be constitutional processes in the international order, there can hardly be any genuine democracy, and certainly no true public opinion. The protection of the right to form opinions and of the sources which make public opinion possible involve the whole question of constitutional liberties. It is, however, an entirely different matter to insist upon pushing them as far as the International Declaration of Human Rights would have done. This declaration, promulgated as an ideal doctrine by the United Nations, goes beyond existing practices of the most advanced constitutional states and may serve as an apple of discord to be thrown by the Soviet bloc for propaganda purposes. The last state in the world to achieve reality for the Declaration on Human Rights would be Stalinist Russia, which makes the greatest propagandistic use of them.*

For purposes of foreign policy, however, the democratic electorate can hardly insist upon more than programmatic responsibility under a broad mandate to the government and

---

* This summary view is expanded by the following quotation from W. Y. Elliott and N. A. McDonald's, *Western Political Heritage* (Copyright 1949 by Prentice-Hall, Inc., New York; reprinted by permission of the publisher), p. 993: "The test of the extent of the *moral community* on which the United Nations might rest is to be found most clearly in the concept of human rights. It is obvious that the totalitarian system of Russia cannot in fact admit any genuine conception of civil liberties and that its attitude in all the meetings of the Human Rights Commission of the Economic and Social Council of the United Nations was dictated by this fact. The effort to work out principles finally resulted in a broad statement or a 'declaration' which went considerably farther than there would be any prospect of getting agreement from the Soviet system or the countries under its control. On their part, they insisted on putting in as many statements of 'rights' as would prove embarrassing to countries with minority problems of either a national, religious, or economic character. This particularly characterized the effort to draft an actual Covenant on Human Rights and made that document too 'watered down' to represent any real progress."

the powers of open criticism with all the free institutions necessary to that end. To expect public opinion to operate directly and unilaterally even within a single system (through referenda or similar devices) on all the major issues is patently absurd. On the other hand, to mobilize its support by processes which would extend the rule of law is a major part of the strategy of the United Nations and of the states adhering to the objectives of the United Nations Charter.

VI

THE POLITICAL PARTY AS AN INTEGRATING FACTOR IN THE FORMULATION AND CONTROL OF FOREIGN POLICY

THE PARTY SYSTEM, which had been almost unappreciated by the Founding Fathers, has come to be our main contemporary reliance for achieving unified policy and "programmatic" responsibility, so vital to creating the dynamics of national unity in world leadership. The structure of all modern types of democratic government has made parties a necessity in the coordination of policy, and the party mechanism is normally expected to resolve executive-legislative deadlocks. Yet the startling paradox exists that all basic foreign policies either require parties to transcend partisanship and to achieve bipartisan support, or, alternatively, to have such overwhelming party superiority as to make opposition unimportant and democracy therefore tenuous or unreal.

OBSERVATIONS ON POLITICAL PARTIES

We believe that the basic elements of foreign policy require bipartisan support in order to present a calculable, secure, and united front to a world where our survival depends upon carrying along as much allied support as possible. Even more important is the breadth and depth of support for foreign policy within the nation. This, too, requires active support and conviction beyond the limitations of party. It requires, especially, a willingness on the part of both parties not to make foreign policy in its main outlines a political issue. This requires consultation with the opposite party and great self-restraint by both parties—often beyond the limits of partisan advantage.

The nature of "party" itself in the enforcement of democratic responsibility does not mean, as some theorists—and practitioners—seem to demand, that each party should oppose everything that the other party supports. The basis of "party" does not require a theory of continuous scrimmages on all questions, whether it rests on Burke's definition and the English tradition, or on variations on the same theme in the American tradition (which emphasize the party as a broker of opinions, a method for resolving sectional and interest group conflicts, and a way of maintaining a national alignment). Indeed, in a healthy democracy the range of disagreement between the parties on "fundamentals" tends to approach the vanishing point on constitutional issues and to present very low contours even on economic and so-called "class" issues.

In what modern democracy, for instance, is social security any longer an issue in a basic sense? There may be, and are, vigorous quarrels about socialized medicine and about the range of assistance the state should perform. A similar analysis of fiscal policy indicates agreement of almost equal extent in the broad outlines of compensatory action by the state; though there may be (and are) severe clashes as to whether this action should follow Keynesian lines, rather than the more orthodox views of credit control through fiscal policies relying on private banking and other means of a like nature.

In other words, party alignments are methods of permitting the nation to disagree on some issues but to agree on others, and to enforce responsibility for a high standard of administration on those matters where there is broad agreement. Party discipline in the minority party might actually result in a greater degree of bipartisan agreement, since most of the most determined opposition often comes from factions that could not command the support of their own party. In the last analysis the party usually recognizes that its fate is determined at the polls by the type of candidate it presents and its total record of successful administration as well as policies.

The utility of party discipline in foreign affairs is therefore manifestly less great than is widespread national support. The Chief Executive, in the face which he turns toward the world, must represent a leadership of the American people that transcends partisanship and assumes national support. Today he must become a leader of the free world. In wartime this is always recognized. A tendency, indeed, to damp down criticism of the President may go too far under the feeling that war requires a sort of temporary mandate toward constitutional dictatorship, somewhat on the model of the Roman *"Dictator,"* for its successful conclusion.

But the advantage of party responsibility is that it does assure the stable nucleus of support for issues that to the average voter or Congressman may seem unimportant or peripheral to foreign policy, but that in reality are central to it. For example, without party responsibility, a free vote of the House and the Senate might find a bipartisan alignment supporting some issues of specious or political attractiveness (such as the earlier efforts to force Franco Spain into the Marshall Plan against the wishes of the Organization for European Economic Cooperation) which would be disruptive, perhaps fatal to a whole line of carefully negotiated policy. Party discipline is, therefore, necessary to maintain the coherence and continuity of foreign policy through adequate legislative support. It is also essential in winning popular support by seeing to it that the Administration's policy is defended by effective political spokesmanship.

How can party organization at once achieve an adequate measure of such disciplined support, and, at the same time, sufficiently permit both the necessary freedom for criticism and participation of the opposition in the processes of the formulation of policy to assure bipartisan support? This is the double necessity which party responsibility faces in democratic systems, whether parliamentary or presidential.

The classic theory of party responsibility assumes that two responsible parties will have two points of view and will between them take the principal issues to the people. This process, however, is one that can be maintained only if each of the parties is relatively coherent, and willing to cooperate with the other in conducting public debate over a few major problems. In the United States government, by contrast, there is presently no way to control, by top level agreement, the manner in which issues are shaped up for public discussion. It is an open question as to how much of this is a result of the fact that we elect the President and the Congress for fixed terms independently of each other, and how much it is the effect of our national political habits, and of the ways in which both our legislative and executive branches are organized internally. No doubt there is a reciprocal character to these factors in terms of cause and effect.

SUGGESTED REFORMS OF POLITICAL PARTIES

It is our feeling that none of the proposals emanating from political circles or from professional academic groups aimed at reform of American parties has really grappled with the *basic* problem. Proposals of the character of those made by the American Political Science Association are of real but limited use within the framework of their intent. Still they do not get to the root of the matter.

The general temper of our discussion supports the demand for increased party responsibility and discipline within the American system. How this should be done, however, brought out differing suggestions. One urged basic constitutional reform to give the President the right to call a general election once during his term. This potential right of the President would serve as a disciplinary "whip." Another emphasized the desirability of changing our thinking about the so-called handicaps of the separation of powers, and of somehow "indoctrinating" the public and the politicians with truer ideas of a cooperative relationship between the Executive and the Legislature, and also of educating party opposition to exert responsible self-limitation to this end. Then there was the historian's feeling that the system represented the "natural" development of a culture; that to tinker with its mechanics was relatively superficial; but that adequate political leadership could make any mechanism work and find ways of securing popular support in spite of the lack of party discipline, if not through it.

It was significant that each of these attitudes tended to look with increased tolerance on the contrary position when a question was raised of party action on specific issues, such as Far Eastern policy (the MacArthur incident), armament policy, or the protection of national security without jeopardizing civil liberties. The "constitutional reformers," when faced with immediate and crucial challenges, tended to seek more practicable, even if less basic solutions. The "indoctrination" proponents and the historical "naturalists" tended to favor certain constitutional alternatives, such as four-year terms for Congress, in order to establish the basic power of the President, which neither patronage nor control of central spending, nor party prestige appeared to support adequately.

The "historical-minded," under persuasion of facts, tended to concede that "mechanics" might have some bearing on institutional reforms both at the constitutional and at government levels.

As to party reforms themselves, all recognized the validity of setting up party general staffs, like the British Transport House of the Labour Party; increasing the importance of, or creating, policy committees in both Houses for both parties; providing more systematic consultation between the President as party leader and congressional leaders; and, finally, raising larger "war chests" for continuing operation of the party mechanism between elections, and for supporting candidates who followed the party program or pledged themselves to it.

VII

THE ROLE OF "LEADERS" AND

PROFESSIONALS

OBSERVATIONS ON LEADERS AND
THE PROFESSIONAL SERVICES

Assuming a philosophy of foreign policy, and a structure to carry it out, it is then important to recruit people who understand it and who will operate it "generally." One of the things that should be asked about the structure of government in any democracy is whether it induces good people to serve, both as leaders in the non-professional service and as professional and civil servants. Beyond bringing good people into the government, it is obvious that a good structure could make them more effective.

"LEADERS" AND DEMOCRATIC METHODS

Great political leaders are great political educators. Failures in political leadership are failures in explaining moral and historical necessities to the people. While it is important of course to have leadership that can explain programs, the nub of the problem is still to be able to carry them out. The problem of leadership is to make the dormant masses rise above local political machines. A historian's view generally is that the basic trouble with our foreign policy lies less with the structure of government than with the failure in political education and leadership. Its cure is thought to come not from redesigning structure and procedures, but from improving popular knowledge and understanding of the necessities of policy. Obviously, structural and procedural improvements may contribute considerably to the process of increasing popular understanding, but they can do very little when such increased understanding does not exist.

Such a view is attractive and certainly in part true. But it leads to the difficult and important problem of what may be called either "political prudence" or "political art." Part of the problem of political education depends on the methods by which issues can be presented to the electorate for a choice through elections. Machinery here is important. But to estimate leadership (or to get it) is a matter which involves the more subtle factors of personalities; of estimating the timing, the atmosphere, the psychology of congressional opinion; and quite as much, too, the preparation of a public opinion which will support the greatest possible cooperation on the part of Congress with the desired ends of the Administration. It is clear that in this area personal relations and party leadership hold the key to any realistic approach to solutions that cannot be achieved by mere vote or the following of a formula. Political prudence in such an analysis consists in ascertaining as far as possible whether past evidence reveals patterns of congressional behavior that may be expected under a given set of circumstances, the most useful methods of approaching congressional leaders for support, and of avoiding unnecessary offense to congressional susceptibilities, whether the latter be rational or irrational in character. Political science may add the factor of what different systems of electoral machinery can be expected to produce. But it is, above all, in this factor of human nature in politics that experience and wisdom are the essential guides. The answers may not at all indicate the superiority of timidity as an approach, but they do require prudence. This is necessary in any system. Is an unreasonable degree of it required by our system of its leaders and the public? Are our methods of public education *through party responsibility* adequate?

PROFESSIONAL SERVICES

With respect to our government as a whole we have, until very recently, preferred to concentrate on high theory and legal principles. We have in consequence neglected the grubbier job of creating a disciplined administrative system, quite as much as we have neglected the deeper study of party process.

What is a disciplined organization? It is a corps of men who are trained to work together, with the habits of teamwork, for a common purpose, under responsible leadership. We have such a corps in the armed services. We began in 1924 to develop such a corps in the Foreign Service. But these are specialized corps. A professional specialist, such as a diplomat or a soldier, has to learn some things well, and leave other things to other people. The soldier has to assume the support of the nation in time of war; the diplomat has to assume that the nation has a policy. The new dimension that has developed in our international affairs is beyond the calculus of the soldier or the diplomat as such.

Yet the soldier and the diplomat know that the government has no general corps of civilian administrators who can work under responsible political leadership to develop and execute a comprehensive policy. And the world does not stand still to wait for us to settle our quarrels at home.

This is why the armed services have to take on jobs and make decisions that ought to be left to civilians. This is why we have so little agreement on the proper relationship between the career official—military or civilian—and his political superiors. And this is why a series of imposing studies by outside experts has not straightened out the relationship between the Foreign Service and the Civil Service, and has left both sides suspicious and embittered.

Our plan of organization may still be, for all its faults, better than our system of personnel. Of course, the civil service system today, with all its shortcomings, is infinitely better than the spoils system it replaced. That reform was made when the Congress hit on a simple principle that is the key to the improvement of legislative-executive relations—that it is perfectly constitutional for the Congress to legislate, and to leave administration to the Executive. Accordingly, the Congress decided to deal with personnel by general legislation, and to leave the President responsible for detailed civil service rules and the specific actions taken by his subordinates.

But the "dead hand" of bureaucratic traditionalism, rigidity, and timidity must be recognized where it exists. The general prestige and the specific rewards of public service are still low enough to encourage a great many able men to stay out of the government. Some of the most important positions in our defense mobilization program, for example, are staffed by men who are working part time, or for three or four months, and are serving without compensation. As individuals, they deserve the highest praise for their public spirit and patriotism. But a government is less shrewd or less able to attract or command than it should be if, in the face of an indefinite period of mortal rivalry with aggressive communism, it is willing to guide its economic mobilization in such a haphazard manner.

In two fields our government has set up planned careers for men of ability regardless of their politics. These, of course, are the military and the foreign services. They have attracted a great many men of high ability. On the other hand, they develop a loyalty to a professional specialty that is considerably narrower than our national policy as a whole. This is the obvious reason for the great difficulty that we have had in the unification of our armed forces. It is also the reason for the less conspicuous but equally difficult problem of bringing about greater unity between the Foreign Service and the Civil Service generally.

The Foreign Service is properly proud of the fact that it has been the only civilian service in the United States Government to combine a merit system with a planned career. It could maintain itself as a separate elite corps, with the support of the Foreign Affairs and Foreign Relations Committees of the Congress, as long as diplomacy was regarded as a separate art. But the new dimension of diplomacy brought so much of our domestic politics into international affairs that it became obvious that no self-administered corps could stay on top of the heap. The issue now becomes this—whether the elite corps will be submerged into the routine Civil Service, or whether some new system can be devised to infuse into our federal service the high competence, the non-partisan approach, and the planned careers that have been held up as an ideal by the best members of the Foreign Service. As a Study Group, we are optimistic enough to hope that this can be done without sacrificing the flexibility and the equality of opportunity that have been strong points of American public service. But a danger of destroying the morale and high expertise of the Foreign Service involved in any sweeping change to civil service status of the ordinary type is admitted.

The functional and professional specialization of the Civil Service, and the temporary nature of most government careers, have kept the general Civil Service as such from furnishing any cohesive or unifying influence. As previously noted, the two principal types of career service in the government—the military and the foreign services—develop special points of view of their own or, at the least, are not considered to represent, in their collective opinions, the program of the President and his administration. The non-partisan Civil Service covered most of the remaining positions of the government, including many high positions with great influence on policy. But it remains a collection of individuals, not a cohesive corps, not a hierarchy with an apex.

Alternatives for the organization of the Foreign Service and its relations to the rest of the government and to the State Department proper illustrate a wide variety of views as to what the function of the Foreign Service should be in our system. These differences arise from the fact that the Foreign Service has to try to combine several functions. In the first place, since it must serve abroad, in danger posts, and in difficulty, and since its members are often removed from their families and from familiar territory for very long periods under circumstances that offer less than adequate compensatory pay and allowances, the Foreign Service in the past has had to take on some of the characteristics of a disciplined career service, more or less self-administered. It made up perhaps in morale and in a sense of being "an elite corps" what it lost by having its roots too little planted in American traditions and by not serving the government as a whole rather than the diplomatic machinery in particular. Until relatively recently, on the record of its recruitment, it offered the greatest attraction to sons of wealthy families and to those who preferred to live abroad rather than in the United States, and sometimes to adventurous and imaginative characters. Many a youth has been misled by the opera "Madame Butterfly" into the thought that he might be playing the role of a Pinkerton in a flowering Japan, rather than that of a consul who spends an uninteresting career in filling out papers in some God-forsaken quarter of the globe. It is amazing that more disillusion has not resulted. It did not, again until relatively recently, offer a career leading to the highest diplomatic posts, and it was not integrated into the State Department or the Civil Service as a whole.

This situation has been changed in more recent times by new opportunities and better recruiting methods.

After World War II the Foreign Service, as well as the State Department, picked up all sorts of remnants of war agencies, such as the Foreign Economic Administration. But this was manifestly too much of a good thing in the way of expansion. Apart from the sweeping implications of breaking down all distinctions between the State Department, the Foreign Service, and the rest of the Civil Service, consideration had to be given to the possibility of retaining people in public service who did not wish to be ordered abroad to out-of-the-way posts. It soon became evident that some compromise would have to be worked out which would retain many of the characteristics of the traditional Foreign Service with certain so-called "improvements."

Entry into the Foreign Service has been greatly expanded so that specialists can be admitted at the age of 40 or above without having to go through tedious preparations for a career beginning at about 21, as in the British Service. Furthermore, under recommendations of the Rowe Report, now apparently accepted, a certain freedom of movement will be permitted for those who wish to join the Foreign Service from the State Department.

A limited Foreign Service Reserve has been set up, though this does not have the breadth of coverage that could make it a valuable political adjunct to the Reserve Officers Corps, comparable to the Armed Services Reserve. An approach to this, already initiated, deserves broadening and improvement.

What will emerge from the proposals now before Congress to deal with the reorganization of our foreign representation abroad along the lines recommended by the Brookings Institution becomes a part of the larger problem of whether we are to set up an operating foreign arm of the State Department to control all the civilian authorities of our government abroad, as some members of our Study Group were inclined to recommend. Such an organization would absorb foreign representatives of the Economic Cooperation Administration and of the Technical Aid Missions, along with technical people of other departments. It would take over the civilian activities in Occupied Territories so far as these remain, and would in general act as the overseas arm of the government and combine all the representatives of other agencies, as the Foreign Service did with respect to the representatives abroad of the Department of Commerce.

This would raise particular difficulties with the Departments of Agriculture and the Treasury, who insist on maintaining separate status for their foreign officers as well as direct reporting to the home base, even though these representatives are technically parts of United States missions abroad. There would still, however, be the necessity for distinguishing between an operating arm of the Foreign Service abroad, responsible to an operating overseas set-up, under the Secretary of State but headed by a separate head for Overseas Operations on the one side, and, on the other, a traditional Foreign Service Officer who is an extension of the policy-forming staff area of the State Department as now organized. The experience of the Economic Cooperation Administration has shown that it is not impossible to bring together two such agencies harmoniously as parts of the same mission. This was also the net conclusion drawn from the experience of the Harriman and other special missions during World War II.

The necessity for tackling the problem boldly along some such lines as these was granted; although our agreement on specifics was not unanimous. Emphasis was placed on better methods of recruitment, the kind of personnel to be selected, and improved relations between the professionals and the political leaders. In this respect, it was agreed that capable "generalists" are required in the formulation and conduct of foreign policy. It is relatively easy to get competent technicians and specialists but very difficult indeed to get good "generalists."

Moreover, there is the added difficulty in training in that there are strikingly few courses even in the great universities in the country on such specialized subjects as strategy or the military factors in history. This is a reflection of the failure of liberal democracy to emphasize force as a major factor in world politics and to study the power organization of the world as a reality—noted, lamented, and in some part met by the late Secretary of Defense James Forrestal. This failure has resulted partly from our general cultural context; partly no doubt it is the product of the selection methods of State Department and Foreign Service officials in the past and of an inadequate appreciation of this whole problem in our national policy. It requires a remedy. None of us, however, could see any hope of solving this merely by setting up a public training institute at the undergraduate level, on the theory that we might specialize through a sort of West Point for young and aspiring diplomats.

PART THREE

POWER, PRINCIPLE, AND POLICY

THE PROBLEM of ends and means, as we have seen, takes on a peculiarly sharp form in the conflict between power and principle. The general form of the problem has already been discussed. But we also found this problem to show itself with peculiar clarity in three areas where it takes special and significant shapes.

Does the crucial nature of "security" in a military sense require measures designed to eliminate subversion and espionage and a tightening of general controls over public servants of such a "police-state" nature as to threaten the basic civil liberties essential to democracy? Freedom of communication and movement for all people, and for intellectuals and professional groups especially, is basic to better understanding of genuine community and moral values for a free world. The question of the role of the courts and the protection of civil liberties have both internal and external implications for modern foreign policy. What security policies, immigration controls, and state organizations of covert policy and intelligence are involved in an adequate modern foreign policy? What bearing have court decisions on these facets of the problem? Legislative Acts? Executive policies?

VIII

NATIONAL SECURITY AND
INDIVIDUAL FREEDOM

OBSERVATIONS ON SECURITY AND FREEDOM

IT IS OFTEN ASSUMED that the problem of domestic civil liberties can be separated from the conduct of foreign policy and that internal problems of this order do not necessarily affect the attitude of a nation toward its external threats and responsibilities. A little reflection shows this assumption to be radically false on several grounds.

The first is that the crucial nature of military security, including those factors of secrecy and unified alignment of the national effort, tend to increase the tightening of party lines and of control over political attitudes and governmental proceedings on issues where in ordinary times there is room for great division of opinion and for much freer information on, as well as discussion of, military and strategic matters. Recent loyalty proceedings have been supplemented by even more severe standards for the protection of "security" in public servants. It is not only the elimination of subversion and espionage which is in question. The security program permits the dismissal of public servants whose loyalty is not in question but who are judged to afford a risk of a serious character, including that of the "leak" of public documents of a most secret and important nature. This may occur through mere indiscretion or through various forms of pressure to which the individual may be subjected, or through "association," even associations that have no implications of disloyalty or bad judgment. That this tightening of "security" measures constitutes a threat to the intellectual freedom and development of ideas and their interchange is widely recognized.

International freedom of movement of intellectual and professional groups is outside the immediate scope of this problem, except in so far as association of public servants with known sympathizers to an enemy affords a risk to security. The general cramp that descends on policy-making and criticism through the overclassification of papers and the failure to transmit a needed understanding of the bases and the background of policy even within the government is also increased by the constriction of information that is necessary for intelligent and informed congressional and public support or criticism.

The second major difficulty that is imposed by considerations of national security comes in the internal alignment of political support. If association with those who are critical of certain aspects of the economic order is indentified with association with enemies of the system, there is an increasing resentment on the part of the "liberal" groups and a danger of their throwing unnecessary support to more subversive and real enemies through concern over civil liberties, freedom of speech, and so forth. In the final sense, the world alignment itself is seriously affected by an internal tightening of organizational discipline which may cut off contacts among the groups within this nation who can carry weight with socialists and other left-wing but anti-communist groups abroad and who are the necessary bridge to some understanding with important allies.

It seems important to root out the "controlled" communist and to eliminate his agent or even dupe from governmental office, without terrorizing mere independence of mind. Se-

curity measures for domestic protection against communist
espionage and subversion may be reasonably expected to increase in severity; but it is unlikely that either policy or administration in this area will be devolved upon the military officers, short of national disaster. Dangers to civil liberties are
not likely to arise from the military, despite fears of a so-called
"garrison" state.

These problems involve, therefore, the role of the courts,
of administrative boards and tribunals, and of public opinion
in protecting civil liberties adequately to permit growth of
free discussion and the formulation of responsible opinion. They
involve necessarily, therefore, the protection of legitimate civil
liberties, without which the lines are drawn increasingly between fascist tendencies and communist sympathizers or puppets. Groups tend to align themselves on the one side in terms
of coercive support for everything in the existing order as
against those on the other who demand revolutionary activities and are bent upon overthrowing the entire existing
order. In other words, the healthy middle ground of democracy and the mediating role of the middle class are made increasingly difficult. Sometimes the trend toward coercion is
simply to advocate support for whatever government is in
power, no matter how "rightist" its social and political alignments may be in terms of the political spectrum—for example,
Franco's Spain or Perón's Argentina—as against all leftist
regimes. To produce such an absolute right-left alignment,
with the democracies being forced over to the extreme right
would, of course, be a triumph for Moscow. It would condition
the terms of the struggle favorably for those who pose as
"revolutionaries," though in fact they are the most archaic
and reactionary imperialists. But to move left merely through
tactics of competing with communist parties for "reform" is
equally, if not more, suicidal. They can always outbid a constitutional regime on those terms.

Finally, the restrictions which the legislature may impose on freedom of movement among countries may grow to proportions as serious as those imposed by the original McCarran Bill, where whole categories of groups within nations and, indeed, almost entire nations who are not unfriendly to the purposes of the United States could be classified as inadmissable for entry to the United States. The cutting off of entry to *former* communists, also, no matter how vigorously they now fight Moscow, deprives our nation of one of its most valuable sources of information and potential allies in the struggle of the Cold War.

SUGGESTED REFORMS ON SECURITY AND FREEDOM

We are confronted today by very genuine problems of protecting government secrets and of preventing the undermining of government servants by systematic penetration from Moscow. This has resulted in an almost continuous process of attack by some congressional committees on the loyalty and trustworthiness of government servants in various agencies, particularly in the Department of State. As a consequence, security boards and a Loyalty Review Board have been set up whose decisions influence the entire morale and tone of the government. If they are too lax, they may fall into the error of leaving us vulnerable to penetration. If they are too severe (mainly from fear of congressional reaction and publicity), they may destroy innocent people and inject a creeping paralysis into the exchange of ideas within the government. In no field is this problem more serious than where people are dealing with foreign policy and military security. Nowhere is it more necessary for the specialist and the technician, as well as the maker of policy, to have not only the necessary information, but to be able to check his views with others without being subject to the cramp of "over-classification." Most of all, it is important to retain among advisers of government men of very different views and those who do not always agree with the official policy. Otherwise official policy is likely to be very ill-considered and not to take into account some of the most vital considerations.

There is no easy solution, of course, for these complex problems. In our discussions we did conclude, on the one side, that a stronger protection in terms of judicial review and of due process of law is needed in the operation of the loyalty and security programs. But there was no disposition to challenge either the seriousness of the problem or the need for rooting out the real concealed communists and those really under foreign "party-line" influence within the government. Nor was there much question of the need for more careful government policy on classification of documents and much less reckless use of the higher classifications "secret" and "top secret" (which should imply the most careful protection of all the documents concerned), as well as a screening of personnel who handled such documents, in terms of discretion and care-taking, as well as of loyalty.

There was also a general consensus that the extremes of the McCarran Act did not reach the real and immediate difficulties of dealing with the disciplined core of the communist party, since its major provisions required a year or two to be made effective, except in time of national emergency; while, at the same time, it imposed unnecessary restrictions and dangerous limits on the freedom of movement of groups who were naturally aligned against communism and whose strength, properly enlisted, was essential for the support of the free world.

Finally, in our judgment, we are affording to the enemies of freedom a supreme opportunity for sowing confusion through taking advantage of the faulty security machinery in the opportunity it offers for denunciations from communist-inspired sources as much as from the "McCarthyites." Both attacks interpose delays and impose burdens by inspiring a timidity of action which make the machinery almost unworkable for the purposes for which it was rightly intended. The alignment of the United States with the nations of the free world requires protection of the necessary freedoms in order to operate the United Nations without permitting the abuses of diplomatic status which the Soviet bloc has attempted with regularity.

Some question was raised as to whether over-classification of policy documents, among other things, might not do more harm to the internal unity and efficient functioning of the United States government than would a more relaxed policy in this matter. Soviet intelligence is in general provided with our major "secrets" of a policy nature, if only by our own press. In any case, the difficulties experienced by Russia are more those of interpretation of policy than of acquisition of facts.

It was recognized at the same time, however, that foreign policy today depended more than ever upon adequate intelligence, and that control of genuinely subversive movements and espionage made necessary new machinery and new approaches on the part of democratic governments. That these necessities present dangers cannot be denied. But in a world where survival is at stake, that they could be rejected merely because they impinge upon the processes traditional to democracy in its rather lax policy and administrative organization is hardly tenable.

There is a danger that Congress may help Moscow to secure most of the data and a great deal of intelligence on United States attitudes. Still it is conceivable that hearings, even those of the character previously alluded to ("MacArthur dismissal" and Unification of the Armed Services) may do more good than harm. They tend to dramatize the problems in a manner that leads democracies to understand the challenge to which they must respond and the necessary sacrifices entailed. Their domestic educational value outweighs any danger to secrets— most of which are already well known to Moscow. They also help to make the Soviet rulers understand that we as a nation support our foreign policy and act on it.

IX

THE PROBLEM OF FORCE
IN FOREIGN POLICY

O N THE important matter of the necessary relation between armed force and policy, nothing in the profession of of a soldier—not his training, his tactics, his weapons, his code of war—and nothing in the military policy of any American command, from the battalion to the Joint Chiefs of Staff, is without relevance to policy. Strictly speaking, there is no such thing as a purely military matter, and certainly those areas in which we can speak of a policy unconnected with force are not the important ones.

In this intimate interconnection of force and policy, final priority belongs to policy. This assertion is, in one sense, so obvious as to require no argument: unless battle and conquest are themselves the whole object of the state, we can always as-sert that force is a means and not an end. However, our claim for policy does not imply that in every contest between a diplomat and a soldier, the decision must be for the diplomat. War has its claims, and these claims may be very great. Good and sufficient reasons must be required before the military are ordered to do it the hard way. Yet the principle remains. Force is a servant of policy; the special requirements of war can modify, but cannot reverse, this relationship.

American notions of war were originally that war was a limited but legitimate activity. After World War I, it appeared instead that it was total and illegitimate, except in case of self-defense. It thus became natural to separate policy from the use of force. In peace it was proper to use only the ways of peace, and in war everything was subordinated to victory. Because war was so bad, it was cast out from the realm of policy. It was renounced (Kellogg Pact), or was thought to be controllable (collective security), or avoided like the plague (pacifism in some cases, neutrality in many more). None of these methods prevented World War II; none of them prevented the gradual increase of international tension in a so-called Cold War after 1945. This suggests that it may have been wrong to try to separate the problem of force and policy, and the following propositions are advanced:

War, though terrible in all forms, and very nearly unendurable in its total form, is not the worst of evils. The possibility of war and a willingness to fight are therefore necessary parts of policy.

The sort of interest which may require defense by force cannot be arbitrarily determined, either by setting territorial limits or by prescribing fixed rules of behavior which will inevitably provoke retaliation by force.

Readiness for armed conflict is at all times a part of policy, though force in action is an instrument not generally available to American policy-makers unless there has been a prior act of aggression by an unfriendly party.

Aggression by others, whether against us or against some third party, permits, but does not always require, any use of force which may seem advantageous to American policy. The moral and political value of action under the United Nations must be weighed in all such cases. The moral advantages of consistent, collective action against *all* aggression weighs heavily in any basis for an international order of law. Any departure from this position should be recognized as dictated only by a state of weakness that demands remedy.

Not all force is total force; we must not draw too much from the misleading experience of the two world wars. Force under policy may be strictly limited in shape and scope, and the political objectives of a use of force may be far short of unconditional surrender. This becomes particularly important if unconditional surrender is unattainable, or pointless in policy terms. On the other hand, force must be adequate to prevent a hostile will being imposed upon the United States.

The fact that American policy cannot be the first to resort to war does not mean that American armed forces—fleets and armies in being and purposefully deployed—are in peacetime an unimportant part of policy, for this reason:

A very great part of American policy at present is the development and exhibition of a power balance which will frustrate and deter an aggressor. The creation of such a power balance is a very different thing from preparation for an expected total war, and this difference clearly illustrates the distinction between military policy, considered in and by itself, and military policy considered as a wholly interconnected element of American high politics.

In earlier sections of this paper we have noted that this fundamental connection between policy and power implies a special and greatly increased leadership by the President and his staff, as well as increased coordination between the State and Defense Departments. Within the Defense Department we have found a need for expansion of the powers and activities of the Secretary of Defense. We have also noted that the Congress will deal more effectively with foreign affairs if it can come to think of military men as primarily the servants of policy and not as independent experts in a field all their own. But all of this discussion turned on the assumption that the policy of which power would be a part would be a policy which gave full understanding to the critical importance of military factors in foreign affairs. It may therefore be appropriate here to remark that this understanding is still most imperfectly developed throughout our nation.

The oscillation between faith in abstract principles and reliance on naked force which has characterized our behavior in world affairs until recently is matched by an oscillation in our academic writings between a breast-beating moralism and a chest-thumping (or Machiavellian) *Realpolitik*. And the articulate public tends to divide into those who praise virtue and those who praise strength, both sides seeming to believe that they have found a single and sufficient key to world affairs. It is these public attitudes, quite clearly, which lie behind many of the specific administrative difficulties to which we have called attention in this area. The complex and always imperfect interaction of power, principle, and purpose, as part of one continuous pattern, is a fact of our present life; and in proportion as it is more widely understood, we shall be able to act more effectively. The events of the last five years have greatly increased our understanding of this fact, but much remains to be done. We believe that leadership in understanding and clarifying this inevitable interconnection can come from the Administration, from Congress, and from private citizens.

We emphasize this problem of interconnection because we think it fundamental to the consideration of the more traditional question of "civilian control." We are earnest in our agreement that the civilian must have the last word, but we can understand how little he will command the confidence of soldiers and those who praise soldiers if he does not understand the soldier's great mission and function. We are even tempted to the paradoxical assertion that the danger of the "garrison state" arises more from civilians who undervalue power than from any military group, and we think history stands with us in this opinion.

X

MULTILATERAL DIPLOMACY AND
TECHNIQUES OF ALLIANCE

OBSERVATIONS ON MULTILATERAL DIPLOMACY

THE PERIOD following World War II has seen the emergence of a new phenomenon in the conduct of our national policy, namely, extensive participation by the United States government in multilateral international bodies, the deliberations and decisions of which often involve commitments comparable in importance to those which have traditionally been considered suitable only for treatment by treaty procedure.

The novelty of the multilateral arrangements in which the United States has been participating since the recent war is largely one of degree rather than one of kind, and expresses itself primarily in the following features:

(1) The international bodies in question are permanent or semipermanent, calling for regular or periodic service of representatives and staffs.

(2) The matters dealt with are often of major importance, affecting the broader political and security interests of the United States.

(3) The American representational establishments are necessarily quite elaborate, in some instances considerably exceeding in organizational strength the Washington office from which instructions are received.

(4) In certain instances the United States government may be committed by a majority vote of the body in question.

(5) The mode of operation is such as to make it unavoidable that the United States representative must function at times either on his own initiative or after only the most cursory check with Washington.

The major multilateral arrangements in which the United States has been participating since World War II and which have presented appreciable organizational problems for our government have been the following:

(6) The occupational and control establishments in ex-enemy countries

(7) The Council of Foreign Ministers and other meetings at the foreign minister level.

(8) The major organs of the United Nations and associated organization

(9) The organs of the North Atlantic Treaty Organization

In the case of the occupational-control establishments in ex-enemy countries, the problem has been one of the extent to which the American officials, whose actions in discharging those responsibilities were destined in any event to constitute United States foreign policy in the eyes of the rest of the world, were really controllable by the United States government and in a position to serve as effective instruments of its policy. By history and tradition, the State Department is an advisory body to the President in the formulation of foreign policy, not a source of American colonial administration. For this reason, such a function as military government, or the control of a foreign government, does not fit the pattern; and the tact and good will of individuals had to be called upon to fill a gap for which organizational logic had no ready solution. Fortunately, these qualities have thus far proved adequate to the purpose.

Some question may be raised as to whether our negotiators

were up to using the power of our national position adequately in the quadripartite or tripartite control agencies in Europe. If these occupational-control establishments were to become permanent features of our governmental operation, it could not be said that present arrangements would be satisfactory. Fortunately they have always been thought of as temporary arrangements. While they have lasted longer than was originally hoped, with a very mixed record of accomplishment, they are in some instances in process of dismantlement; and there are favorable prospects for the early disappearance of most of their features. For this reason, the organizational inadequacies which have been involved hardly require study from the standpoint of finding solutions to present specific difficulties. But lessons for a possible future should not be lost.

Occupational-control establishments are by nature in many respects colonial establishments, though complicated by multilateral features. This brings to mind the fact that no system has yet been evolved for an adequate centralization of the responsibility for this broad type of colonial administration within the United States government, or for its effective reconciliation and coordination with the conduct of foreign policy.

The meetings at the foreign minister level, both quadrapartite and tripartite, which have marked the post-hostilities era have proven thus far to be the least problematical of any of the forms of multilateral or supranational authority. In fact, the surprising feature of the foreign minister meetings has been the extent to which it has proved possible for the Secretary of State to speak successfully for the government of the United States as a whole. One of the distinguishing marks of the aftermath of World War II has thus far been the minor role that the treaty instrument has played in shaping the realities of the post-hostilities era. In so far as those realities were not predetermined by the events of the war and the meetings of the heads of state during the war, they have been determined largely by meetings of the foreign ministers. And there can be no question but that many of the decisions taken at these meetings have been fully as important as matters which in the past were regarded as suitable for settlement by treaty. It is noteworthy that such peace treaties as have been concluded have been negotiated at the foreign minister level.

For brief periods, when actually seated at the Foreign Ministers' Council table with his ministerial colleagues, the Secretary is tacitly conceded a status quite different from that which he normally enjoys in Washington. This has enhanced the influence of his office, and has meant that for purposes of negotiation and for as long as negotiations were in progress, the United States government has had a leadership and focal center in foreign affairs within the Executive Branch which it was not prepared to accept at other times. This represents a distinct advantage of the foreign ministers' meetings, from the standpoint of the coordination and centralization of the control of American foreign policy. Of equal interest has been the general acceptance by the Legislative Branch of the peculiar responsibility of the Secretary of State as a negotiator for this country at the foreign minister level.

United States participation in the United Nations involves the assignment of a portion of the policy-making function to a number of people outside the regular and traditional policy-making center of the Department of State—to the representative on the Security Council, to the members of our Delegation to the General Assembly, and to the members of their staffs and the staff of the Bureau of United Nations Affairs in the Department of State. The significance of this is greatly heightened by the marked differences in atmosphere and outlook which often separate these people from the old established divisions of the Department and from the Foreign Service in general.

One feature of this difference is probably the importance

attached in United Nations circles, American and foreign, to the United Nations as an institution, rather than just a forum of diplomacy. Aside from the ideological preconceptions about international organization and world law which people may bring to their work in connection with United Nations affairs, few people can be long associated with United Nations headquarters without being affected by the symbolism and spirit which tend to give it its own meaning and its own institutional existence. The United Nations is the tender shoot of a new phenomenon in international life; the young child of the national state, now helpless in its parents' care but destined some day to become a personality in its own right, to rival and eventually overtake its parents in strength and importance, and finally to outlive them. These people are conscious of having a stake in United Nations activity and in their own part in it beyond the parochial interests of the government which they serve. In this way their interest in that activity comes to rest upon a wider basis than policy thinking in the confined precincts of the Department of State itself.

In addition to this, and closely connected with it, there is a different sense of relationship to the American public and Congress on the part of people engaged in United Nations work than on the part of people in the more traditional phases of American diplomatic activity. There is the feeling in some quarters that those people who represent the United States in the United Nations have a different and closer bond with the American public, and a greater duty to speak for the public directly, than would normally be felt by the traditional apparatus of the Department of State and the Foreign Service. While it is dangerous to generalize, there is surely a certain feeling on the part of many of the foreign delegations that the United States government, personified by such symbols as the "State Department" and the "Pentagon," is more reactionary, more "imperialistic," and more sinister than the people for whom it speaks. If, therefore, it can be demonstrated to them that the American Mission to the United Nations speaks for the country at large—that it voices, in other words, the feelings of the man in the street who is innocent of the intrigues and plots of government—foreign delegations, it is assumed, are quicker than they would otherwise be to respond to American impulses and suggestions. For Americans at the United Nations this puts a premium on demonstrating the legitimacy of their urgings by pointing to their origin in popular feeling and by claiming a special intimacy with the public mind.

The United Nations, under any realistic appraisal, is in fact still the instrument of national policies. It is not an institution in itself at this stage of its development.

One cannot escape the suspicion here, as in the case of the Occupational Commanders, that Congress is apt to be indulgent for the very reason of its awareness that those representatives are in part independent figures. On the record Congress welcomes this centrifugal diffusion of the policy-making function away from a center—namely, the Department of State—which it has often suspected of being conspiratorial, unresponsive to congressional feelings, and unrepresentative of the outlooks and attitudes of the broader American public. There is something of the "divide in order to conquer" attitude in congressional indulgence to this fissiparous trend.

The North Atlantic Treaty is ostensibly a treaty of alliance. In that sense it is unusual, though not unprecedented, in American experience. Actually it is much more than that, far-reaching and revolutionary in its implications for the conduct of our government's foreign policy—an agreement among a group of governments to collaborate, through established permanent and intermittently functioning bodies, on a considerable variety of the facets of national policy, military, political and economic. It involves not simply a single forum for multilateral deliberation and decision but a considerable number of standing organizations, linked by special bonds of common interest to a variety of authorities and organizational units within the United States government, and capable of taking actions which have important implications for the whole of our national government.

Worthy of note is the limitation on the power of the Secretary of State to conduct foreign relations through the agency of the North Atlantic Treaty Organization bodies, except as this may be compatible with the military policy of the Joint Chiefs of Staff—a situation strongly reminiscent of the position of the Department of State in World War II.

A second point which stands out in arrangements for American participation in the North Atlantic Treaty Organization is the remoteness of the military command from the ostensible crown of the organization—the Council and its body of deputies. A new political community and command have intervened.

In addition to all this there is a further factor, probably more important than those mentioned above, the personal prestige of General Eisenhower himself and the obvious extent to which successful military collaboration among members of the Pact has depended on his personal qualities and moral authority. Even so, General Eisenhower has made no secret of his own analysis that greater political unity of command is essential to his success. It is not so easy as when Franklin D. Roosevelt and Churchill could settle policy.

What this adds up to, so far as the United States government is concerned, is that the entire military phase of the operation of this treaty will be handled somewhere between the Joint Chiefs of Staff and General Eisenhower, and most of it directly, without participation of the State Department. For reconciliation of possible differences and, above all, for final choice between genuinely conflicting alternatives, there has been no convenient and effective authority within the United

States government up to the present. Even for so limited a sphere as the allocation of foreign aid in weapons and economic aid, the I.S.A.C. (International Security Affairs Committee) under Department of State chairmanship proved too weak. The new legislation passed in October, 1951, attempts to remedy this by putting the Director of Mutual Security into the Executive Office of the President, somewhat on the model of the Office of Defense Mobilization.

This also brings up the question of the top forum for political contact between the members of the Pact. While the instrument itself is ostensibly a military alliance, and while even Article II mentions the coordination only of the "international economic policies" of the members, it is obvious that the attempt to collaborate in military and economic matters will raise a host of problems highly political in nature. It will be possible to dispose of these satisfactorily only against a background of close political intimacy among leading members of the Pact. Without an organ of at least more continuous personal consultation and united political support, this is difficult, at best.

The main danger will be that the importance of a high degree of political intimacy and accord and an effective working basis for political decision among the paramount members will not be fully appreciated on the American side; that we will tend to view the North Atlantic Treaty Organization machinery as an adequate substitute for diplomacy. As we have seen above, this is precisely the function it cannot fulfill. But diplomacy itself will depend on unifying political support to make possible any real unity of command.

If we make the error of mistaking the present dream for a reality, the Pact can easily become a form of shackles on American policy under which only the military interest can find full expression. Thus if the North Atlantic Treaty Organization is not overshadowed by close and constant political collaboration with our main North Atlantic partners on a high and somewhat exclusive level, it may produce organizational pressures which will have a distorting effect on the conduct of national policy in Washington. But again we must note that to achieve this requisite degree of informal political association with other members of the Atlantic Pact group would call for a more gathered and disciplined control of the conduct of national policy than exists anywhere in our government under present circumstances. It also calls for organs of high level consultation and cooperation that do not exist. Can they be created?

The American legislative interest in the North Atlantic Treaty Organization appears to be satisfied in large measure by precisely those features in the arrangement which are the primary contributors to diffusion of responsibility as far as handling the American end of the arrangement is concerned, and notably by the prestige and influence of General Eisenhower himself. This bears out the striking fact already demonstrated that the Congress feels more comfortable in relying on the authority and judgment of an American official geographically and bureaucratically remote from the formal center of the conduct of American foreign policy (even when this official can be, in his international position—as General Eisenhower described himself—only "one-twelfth American") than it does in relying on the regular channels for formulation and conduct of policy. Again, in this instance, the price of legislative acceptance seems to be a drastic decentralization of executive authority. Whatever else may be involved, it is clear that American legislators believe in men, not in organizations. Actually none who looks at the alarming "cumbersomeness" and "complicatedness" of the organizational growths which seem to accompany all the efforts of the western democracies to find answers to their common problems can feel that this attitude is wholly without justification. A man is at least a symbol, around which unifying forces and loyalties may grow.

The sovereign state in international relations is only theoretically completely free. In practical fact it exists and acts in a whole pattern of obligations and mutuality with other nations. No nation grows so great that it can afford to forget this.

Historically, democracy has found it difficult to survive a long and continuous state of alert. The threat of total war produces a new kind of "alert." Modern democracies have therefore sought to escape long sustained mobilization by taking recourse to limiting force and to "outlawing aggression" through international organization.

One view is that the channeling of a highly significant portion of our diplomatic business through multilateral and supranational bodies does not call for any new organizational arrangements in the United States government which were not already called for by the ordinary problems of the conduct of foreign policy; but it does make the need for those changes much more pressing and much more urgent.

Another view is that United States participation in the United Nations radically alters the whole governmental organizational problem for the control of foreign policy.

Multilateral diplomacy is marked by a codification process as a result of being subject to an agenda, debate, and a formal vote. These require a degree of consistency, clarity, and explainability that point toward logic and rigidity. The single most important check on multilateral diplomacy is the recourse to bilateral diplomacy. In this connection it must be remembered that the United Nations is not an end in itself. It is simply one of the instruments of national policy until such time as it comes to be a more real and ultimate moral community than the nations comprising it.

The most significant fact about multilateral international organization as a forum for the transaction of United States government business is that it involves representational establishments abroad in many instances more imposing in point of sheer organizational weight, physical pomp, and appeal to the public imagination than a Cabinet office in this country. Manned by persons who are public figures in their own right before the eyes of the American people, these establishments attain a significance far beyond that of the diplomatic missions which our government has traditionally maintained—a significance which in the present circumstances makes it idle to suppose that they might serve only as the instruments of Washington. Remote from the mill wheels of the Department of State, often at odds with Department thinking, well-equipped to appeal to the imagination—and sometimes the self-esteem—of the individual legislator, yet unhampered by the necessity of maintaining prolonged and wearisome familiarity with him, the leading figures of these distant and slightly mythical representational establishments are well adapted to serve as escape hatches for the feelings of legislators or private citizens irritated by the occupational mannerisms of the Department of State, frustrated by its congenital caution and moderation, and left dissatisfied by its lack of showmanship and its unwillingness to over-simplify. To all this must be added the extent to which the representational establishments can, and sometimes do, provide a means of exit from the dilemmas of partisanship in foreign policy—a means of supporting things the country is doing without seeming to support the President or the Administration. The obverse, of course, is that they may also provide a source of material or inspiration for political attacks on the handling of foreign policy at the Washington end. In this curious way, the diffusion of executive responsibility for the conduct of foreign policy serves purposes left unserved, and answers needs left unsatisfied, by the traditional organizational setup of our government as it is today. Eyes turn to the United Nations in New York for very varying reasons.

SUGGESTED REFORMS ON MULTILATERAL DIPLOMACY

The sheer number of American officials involved, and the geometric multiplication of their mutual interrelationships call upon official Washington for an amount of centralization, direction, and coordination of policy and action out of all proportion to anything demanded by the simpler problems and organizational forms of the past.

The United States is approaching a ceiling on international organization beyond which it cannot go without radical change in its sovereign position. This ceiling is set by the limits of what any one man can do at the top of the structure. It has been said, perhaps with undue bitterness, that there are now many organizational "pyramids" that could function just as well bottomside up, except that the typing would not be so well done! If the North Atlantic Treaty Organization were to grow into a supergovernment, it would sooner or later come up against a "sonic barrier," to borrow a scientific term, and once this "sonic barrier" was passed, everything would change, because sovereignty goes with a lurch when it goes. A true community, with all its organs of growth (or, alternatively, a coercive empire) is needed to create a world order. Even an Atlantic Community must find the reality of its community at a deeper level before it can be translated successfully into the most primitive political structure for defense.

PART FOUR

SUMMARY OF SUGGESTIONS
AND CONCLUSIONS

XI

SUMMARY OF SUGGESTED REFORMS—
CONSTITUTIONAL, POLITICAL,
AND ADMINISTRATIVE

THE FOREGOING chapters have demonstrated that the United States government had taken on world-wide responsibilities before it learned to organize its own affairs in a disciplined, coordinated, and responsible manner. Irresponsibility and lack of internal coordination now threaten to cancel out its great power.

Regardless of what specific methods of reform seemed most persuasive to us individually, as a Group we agreed without question on (a) the new importance of associating congressional leadership with the Executive Branch in the formulation of policy; (b) the importance of giving the President enough leverage to overcome the particularist tendencies of executive departments; (c) the importance of associating department heads, and departments generally, with the President and his office in the formulation of policy; and (d) the importance of giving the President adequate authority and staff for this purpose.

Influences in our constitutional or administrative system that now work in favor of an uncoordinated, undisciplined, and irresponsible national policy are to be found in: the separation of powers; the separation of the several public service careers (military, foreign, civil); the dependence on, or responsiveness to, local and minority pressures or special interests shown by Congressmen and congressional committees, as well as their independence of party or executive leadership; the tendency of party organization to concentrate on administrative patronage rather than on broad policies; the exposure of the process of policy formulation to so much publicity and personal pressure from inside and outside that it undermines the integrity of the administrative system; a great deal of internal legalism within the administrative system which leads bureaus to act as if they were private corporations with the right to sue their jurisdictional rivals.

On the other hand, influences in our constitutional or administrative system that now work in favor of a coordinated and responsible foreign policy are to be found in: the fixed tenure of the President; the public's confidence in the President's ability to manage the Executive Branch; the pressure for cessation of the "guerrilla warfare" between the Executive and Legislative Branches under the threat to our survival; the President's constitutional authority over appointments and over foreign and military affairs; the twentieth-century tendency of the Congress to delegate to the President the duty of formulating policy for congressional determination (as in the Budget, the Economic Report, the Foreign Aid Programs); the rudiments of discipline within the party system on basic elements of foreign policy; the development of staff assistance to the President in the growth of the Executive Office; some improvement in the career services.

POINTS OF AGREEMENT ON
POLITICAL STRUCTURE

While our agreement stopped short of supporting any sweeping adoption of the general election device, we did reach a general consensus of support for the following more limited steps in the direction of constitutional reform:

(1) An amendment providing for ratification of treaties by an absolute majority of both Houses instead of a two-thirds vote of the Senate.

(2) A four-year term for members of the House of Representatives, concurrent with the term of the President. This would lessen the perpetual pressure on representatives for reelection, emphasize their election on issues raised in the presidential campaign, and increase their independence of local pressures and bosses.

(3) An item veto power, such as many state governors now possess, to permit the President to reject riders to important money bills to prevent expenditures for local pork-barrel projects.

(4) An amendment to change the system of electing the President in order to divide present electoral votes of each state among the parties in proportion to the number of votes cast.

(5) With somewhat less certainty, we urge the possible advantages of weighting the presidential election and the power of executive leadership in the Congress by some measure of representation of the President's Cabinet in the legislative process. This would involve an amendment to permit the President to select a specific number of his Cabinet members or heads of agencies to sit with voting rights and to participate at their pleasure in deliberations at the House and Senate.

As was indicated earlier (pages 60–61), we were too divided on more sweeping proposals to do more than agree that these deserve more study than has been given by students of the American system. We call attention particularly to proposals for a constitutional convention and to specific amendments giving the President power to call a general election.

It is our considered opinion that without reforms of the order on which we reached general agreement, steps toward increasing party discipline through educating Congress and the public to a more responsible attitude in support of national policies as opposed to separate interests were not likely to be very much furthered by the commonly advocated devices. These devices would be of limited use and they are worth attempting as far as they go: setting up more continuous and better-staffed policy-forming agencies for the political parties themselves; greater use of party funds on a national basis; operation of policy committees in both Houses to attempt the integration of party attitudes—administration and opposition—particularly to insure more responsible party action on foreign policy.

We recognized that such methods afford no substitute for skillful political leadership on the part of the President and the cultivation of widespread popular support that in foreign policy must transcend party discipline. Only by this type of leadership and political skill can the separation of powers be made workable. The present party mechanism for the selection of Presidents is far from affording a guarantee that the best talents available will always be produced at the presidential level. Nor does there seem to be any genuine prospect for removing in Congress obstacles like seniority and the jurisdictional strength of congressional committees, operating often, at present, in terms of particular areas of economic interest for which the committees act more as spokesmen for the parties' interests than as public arbiters.

EXECUTIVE ORGANIZATION

Given these difficulties and the necessity of somehow coping with them, it seems clear that the Executive Branch must be strengthened in its functional and internal organization, quite apart from the problem of the nature and personality of presidential leadership.

The logic of administrative integration has created a staff in the Executive Office of the President running into the hundreds, if one includes only the smaller offices and secretariats, and over a thousand, if one includes the Bureau of the Budget and the National Security Resources Board. The growth from President Hoover's day has been at least fivefold. It has been produced primarily by the need for better management supervision of the federal government's vast structure and sprawling organization. This expansion of the President's direct staff arm has come also from the need for policy integration in such obvious areas as those covered by the National Security Council, the Office of Defense Mobilization, and the Harriman Office for coordinating foreign policy, which have paralleled a great enlargement of the staff of the White House itself.

According to our analysis, the lifting of foreign policy coordination to the presidential level was inevitable, because of the range of domestic issues, as well as domestic politics, which foreign policy now affects. Our analysis leads us also to advocate strengthening the Department of State itself and extending its control over some operating functions like information and the coordination of foreign aid and military aid programs, as well as the civilian aspects of occupation policy. We further suggest the possibility at this time of setting up a separate operating arm of sub-Cabinet status in the State Department to bring together these operating functions, leaving the existing Department of State as a policy staff arm and integrating both aspects under the Secretary. Aside from the present political weakness of the Department of State, the scheme seems sound in the logic of organizational responsibility. We agree that if the Department is not to be so reorganized, there should be a single agency to do what is now done by the Economic Cooperation Administration, the operating aspects of the Technical Assistance Program, and any present phases of economic warfare, including foreign procurement and export control. The relations of such an agency, broader in functions than the Mutual Security Agency, to the State Department and to the Office of Defense Mobilization would present problems. If it were organized as a separate agency with Cabinet status, it should be guided on foreign policy by the State Department and on mobilization requirements by the Office of Defense Mobilization.

In our view, the National Security Council is a distinct step forward in the direction of bringing together the main elements needed in the making and implementing of foreign policy. Yet it shows the difficulties of any secretarial staff agency in multiplying papers reflecting watered-down compromises, instead of reaching and carrying out basic and clear decisions. Mr. Harriman's present position, with a staff outside the National Security Council staff, and the former International Security Affairs Council organization in the State Department present in different ways anomalous organizational developments, combining operational and staff functions, without clear lines of responsibilities.

We also agree on the need for integrating all aspects of staff work on executive management and policy at the White House level, with the help of a single executive assistant to the President (who might be called, as the Hoover Commission did call him, a "Secretary"). We disagree, however, as to the exact nature of this role. Some members are inclined to think that this is more than a merely secretarial function of clearance, reporting, and scrutiny of agenda. The allocation of jurisdictional functions among the executive office agencies requires a figure who would more nearly assume the role of "Assistant President." If such were the case, he would be essentially the political and personal choice of the President, on the model of Harry Hopkins. Others doubt the possibility of having any one man act for the President in this high general level of policy and administrative control. A permanent Chief-Secretary for the Executive Office would be needed, *in addition,* that is, with or without the single "Assistant President." This official should be permanent and non-political—a caretaker, not a policy-maker

The unification of the Armed Forces in the executive department suggests a possible alternative to the single "Assistant President" type of solution. This would be to raise six or eight Cabinet posts to a sort of super-Cabinet level along the lines suggested in England in 1918 by the Haldane Commission. In effect, what Wilson, for the Office of Defense Mobilization, and Harriman, for the coordination of foreign aid, and Secretary Lovett, for the Defense Department, are doing might be further expanded by having the Director of the Budget assume functions similar to those of the British Treasury in control of personnel and promotion policies of the government. The Treasury Department would function as the over-all fiscal and economic coordinating agency, with the Departments of Commerce, Agriculture, and Labor brought together as a sort of congeries of the main elements of the civilian economy. Each grouping of agencies would be under a single super-Cabinet head.

The difficulty with this solution is practical politics, which makes impossible the securing of effective Cabinet officials without giving Cabinet rank, and which makes useless any executive consolidations that are not supported by parallel changes in the organization and procedures of the Congress. But its logic seems quite good; and a Cabinet along these lines might be served by a secretariat which could be an expansion of the present National Security Council.

The coordination of intelligence services, too, has made considerable strides through the present setup of the Central Intelligence Agency and its tie-in with the National Security Council. Since the assumptions on which all policy must rest are a proper function of the deeper analysis of over-all intelligence, it is obvious that this aspect of government now becomes critical to the success of a foreign policy and, indeed, to the nation's survival. The level of the direction and the qualities of the intelligence services are therefore crucial to all the hopes for better organized, formulated, and controlled foreign policy.

We also urge that no modern state can function effectively without better centralization of its information services. Despite all the natural reluctance of a democracy to have such an office, a permanent office of information along the lines of the wartime Office of War Information would be useful, not to manufacture information but simply to coordinate it. The uncoordinated character of present information and propaganda methods contributes seriously to popular confusion. No doubt the foreign aspects of this office could be separated and put under the State Department, since they fall into the realm of psychological warfare. But there is an interesting question as to whether the Department itself properly conceives the integrating tie-in of information at home and abroad, or can command services of that order. One method of permitting this would be to have the information program raised to the level of a sub-department under the Department of State, to parallel the proposed sub-department for foreign operations.

REORGANIZATION OF CONGRESS FOR BETTER LEGISLATIVE-EXECUTIVE RELATIONS ON FOREIGN POLICY

With respect to foreign policy, we recognize that the initiative properly belongs to the President and that the Executive must take steps to improve the liaison with Congress and the informal organization of all matters that are primarily aspects of foreign policy in its broadest sense.

In the matter of liaison with Congress, however, it seems to us that formal machinery of the type of legislative-executive councils would be contrary to the logic of the American system, so long as Congress remains beyond the disciplinary reach of the President in the organization of its committees, their jurisdiction, and the organization of congressional policy and procedure in general. It seems necessary, in short, for the President to choose his own methods of contact with Congress, taking into account the party complexion of Congress and the personalities, rather than merely the official positions of the members of the House and Senate with whom it is necessary to deal.

It seems evident that greater use could be made of select and special committees to broaden the inquiries and to deepen the understanding of Congress, and that inquests by both the Armed Services Committees and the Foreign Relations and Foreign Affairs Committees could often be jointly held with profit and saving of time. But so long as both the House and the Senate contain numerous committees whose impact on foreign affairs is direct and often critical—as, for example, the Appropriations, the Rules, the Judiciary, and the Interstate and Foreign Commerce Committees, the Committee on Executive Expenditures, the Banking and Currency Committees, and even the Committees on Agriculture—it seems impossible to work out any over-all representation of Congress which could assure the Executive of an advance commitment, or even adequately keep the great bulk of House and Senate membership currently and directly informed.

In the light of these facts about the nature of our system, the informal conferences which the President and the Secretary of State are in the habit of having with congressional leaders and with key members might be expanded, but hardly institutionalized.

Nor would the question period, as suggested by Senator Kefauver and others, offer an acceptable solution. If this were

to be made effective as a regular part of parliamentary procedure in our system—where the Senate has, if anything, superior
powers to the House—the Secretary of State and the Secretary
of Defense and probably other Cabinet members affected by
foreign policy issues would have to appear before both Houses
in turn. Inability of the Cabinet members to control questions
and to intervene actively in actual debates which would
develop the interpretation of their answers presents further
difficulties. There is the possibility, too, that loyalty of Cabinet
members to the President might be undermined by a desire to
please Congress and build up a personal following.

Alternative solutions, such as the appearance of Secretary
Acheson before the entire Congress in an informal session,
carrying Secretary Hull's precedent further by answering
questions, are worth further exploration. There, too, the cooperation of the Senate and the House leadership in the
presentation of questions which are relevant and the limitations on freedom of members to force the line of questioning in
particular directions offer problems. Informal hearings present
difficulties of control.

Another alternative appears in the form in which the grand
inquest on the removal of MacArthur was framed. There
executive sessions, which nevertheless permitted an open record of major parts of the testimony, were held by the Senate
Committees on Foreign Relations and Armed Services jointly.
All Senators were permitted to appear, but the direct right
to ask questions was limited to members of the two committees.
The House Foreign Affairs Committee had attempted to open
its sessions on the Marshall aid program to other members of
the House, who were free to ask questions and to participate
in the discussions. This method had more limited results, and
the Senate method appeared to be a more effective way of
securing general participation under strict controls of commit-

tee procedure. The sheer size of the House of Representatives, however, precludes anything like as effective an inquiry as is possible to the Senate through general participation of all its members.

Once more, in short, the lack of a unifying frame of responsibility of the Executive and Congress mutually dictates severe limits on the possibility of a broadly shared participation in the legislative aspects of policy. But to attribute this difficulty solely to mechanics is fallacious in the extreme. In the British system the strict limits of parliamentary inquiries into matters affecting foreign policy and the general framework of relying upon the Foreign Secretary for foreign affairs under a mandate of Cabinet control and general parliamentary responsibility certainly does not permit a wide or thorough participation by the legislature in great issues of foreign policy. Reliance on a selected team for handling the national interests, subject only to the pressures of opinion and parliamentary debate, characterize the British model.

VALIDITY OF CONTROL OF FOREIGN POLICY
BY PUBLIC OPINION

Beyond the question of congressional control lies, of course, the major issue of responsibility to national opinion and the questions that this raises as to the adequacy of information channels and the organization of the public itself for appropriate responses. No one who examines the real workings of the American system can fail to be impressed by the massive organization of information that is available to those who exhibit a genuine interest in foreign affairs. Radio commentators and television now supplement the enormous range of news channels, specialized journals, and the like. If the public daily press gives relatively inadequate coverage to the basic problems of our foreign policy, perhaps this may be a response to reader interest quite as much as a failing of responsibility on the part of the press.

Beyond the information media lie the great channels of dissemination and for debate of these issues in the rich associational life in the United States, through pressure groups and propaganda associations, and citizens' service clubs. What are often called pressure groups—for example, the organized representatives of labor, of business, of agriculture, and the like—participate in various ways in advisory capacities and are kept informed on a special basis on the major aspects of our foreign policy in which they profess interest. The attitude of the United Automobile Workers, for instance, or of the farm organizations, may be critical for the success of the Marshall proposals in quite as great a degree as the attitude of the Chamber of Commerce of the United States or similar organizations. The same thing may be said of the attitude of these groups toward rearmament and toward the major issues of foreign policy itself, for example, our participation in the North Atlantic Treaty Organization, or our basis for settlement in the Far East.

Important propaganda associations, if they may be so termed, concerned in pressing for solutions in foreign policy along the lines of moral attitudes, also carry a very heavy weight in the whole operation of the American system. Representation of the organized religions are flanked by special organizations like the William Allen White Committee to Aid the Allies, or the Stimson-Patterson Committee for the Marshall Plan, or the Committee on the Present Danger.

Serving the informational and sometimes the propaganda efforts of varying groups there is a great range of associations, some of a specialized order like the Council on Foreign Relations, the Foreign Policy Association, the World Federalists, the Atlantic Union Committee, and the various professional associations, most of them equipped with publications and research staffs. The Committee on Economic Development, the National Planning Association, and such groups as the Twentieth Century Fund and the Social Science Research Council. the Brookings Institution and the various foundations comprise a research mechanism unparalleled in depth and range. There can be no complaint about the *volume*, at least, of information available to the people; though there may be real question as to the incisiveness of the analyses and the impact of these specialized groups on the level of mass opinion.

We know of no formula for improvement here, unless it be more intelligent effort.

POWER, PRINCIPLE, AND POLICY

In the area of *over-all national interest,* the military and political aspects of foreign policy are indistinguishable. Both are concerned with the way in which the government binds itself. The instruments of coercion and of persuasion are in fact a single corpus, even if broken down administratively into two major departments, with many subdivisions. In addition, the framing of economic policy, through the Council of Economic Advisers, is a part of the same area of "national interest," in which the military and political aspects are indistinguishable. Beyond the merging at the presidential level of these three fundamental elements of foreign policy in the concept of "national interest," the control over foreign policy tends to shift to the Congress at about the bureau level. But in any event, there is no reason to break down the conduct of the national interest into war and peace compartments. In this area whatever is or is not done is an act of foreign policy; diplomacy is an empty vessel without content. It becomes only a method of expressing a nuisance value. The real content is to be found in what backs up the national interest position.

As no magic formula is available for the relations of democratic leadership to public opinion and to the organized control and responsibility of parties, neither is there an obvious balance that can be struck between security and freedom. Here again is a dilemma with which one must live, exercising some degree of patience and wisdom aimed at its resolution. Our agreements were not difficult to reach on general principles:

It is necessary to tighten up security and loyalty checks over public servants in particular, but there should also be the protection of due process of law and a less timid enforcement of the protections which such a review would involve. That the Communist Party itself should be dealt with as a conspiratorial organization aimed at the overthrow of the state met general assent; but this did not carry with it the assumption that "once a Communist always a Communist," or a policy denying the rights of citizenship to any except controlled party members who rendered voluntary allegiance to Moscow's dictates. There is also the need of protection of a system of discretion and internal responsibility in the administration of these procedures.

Implementation of these policies requires a strengthening of judicial review on behalf of individuals as well as of organizations and imposes policy limitations upon such unadministrable efforts as branding whole nations out of bounds for immigration purposes, as set forth in the first McCarran Bill.

The impact of panicky action of this kind on our foreign relations is recognized and deplored. At the same time, it is also recognized that the excesses of pseudo-liberalism which had been unwilling to see a threat to public safety in the activities of controlled communists had helped to produce the extremes of reaction.

However difficult the assignment of military participation in the formation of foreign policy may be, the proper role of force should be recognized and related to democratic policy in peace

as well as in war. Civilian control as a proper doctrine of
democracy might be readily agreed to. But what, on the other
hand, are the proper professional duties of the military and
how should military responsibility be recognized and im-
·plemented in the formation of policy?

Our discussions brought out fears of too ready acceptance
on the part of Congress of professional military views where
a more complex high policy was in question. Especial concern
was voiced over the peculiarly sacrosanct ("ecclesiastical")
position of the Joint Chiefs of Staff. On the other hand, some
members felt strongly that there was not a sufficient recognition of military advice and estimate of the power situation with
which the nation is actually confronted, either in the fundamental act of budget-making or the assumption of responsibilities through international commitments. Civilian control, for
example, means that Franklin D. Roosevelt could quite properly
disregard the advice of his theatre commanders, especially that
of his naval commander, by confining the fleet at Pearl Harbor,
if one takes into account the necessity for taking certain military
risks in the larger aspects of power diplomacy.

There was deep-seated clash in the understanding of the
connection between politics and strategy in the relationship
between General MacArthur in the field and his military and
political superiors in Washington. There was further difficulty
over the relationship of an American commander to the United
Nations in an undertaking as novel as it was difficult. The
reflection of these difficulties was shown in the congressional
attitude on the dismissal of MacArthur.

We urge the need for greater interchange, even allowing for
present improvements, in the training of civilian policy-makers
in military matters, and of military officers in the background
of policy. This implies a much more continuous and specialized
career in their work on the part of the military arms than is at
present afforded by existing procedures in selection, promotion,

and assignment under a rotation policy for staff duties. A broadening of fundamental training at the military academies and war colleges has already taken place and, in our judgment, should be pushed even further. This is not to say that putting a military uniform on a man produces especial competence. Rather it is recognition of the need for highly professional training to assure discipline and proper military expertise, even in fighting services of highly technical character.

MULTILATERAL OBLIGATIONS

Though we differ somewhat among ourselves as to the relative importance of maintaining a free hand in terms of ultimate national security as opposed to accepting the procedures and actions of the United Nations as "world law," we unite in recognition of the basic change which multilateral organizations has imposed upon the character and methods of diplomacy—particularly for the United States. This adds a new dimension to the training of diplomats and the complications of politics.

Procedurally considered, there is no doubt that "multilateralism" imposes new responsibilities on those who form foreign policy. They must look not only to the difficult task of carrying Congress along, but also to the necessity of persuading a majority of the United Nations. The degree of initiative and discretion allowed the United States delegates to United Nations organs in some measure reflects views as to whether agreement on the international plane is more important than coherent and adequate "national-interest" policy.

Such attitudes are bound to be reflected in the size and nature of the burden which the United States carries in the field of foreign aid; in supporting international conferences of every type, including UNESCO; and in the relative emphasis placed upon strengthening allies rather than looking primarily to our own defenses.

We are agreed on the utopian and illusory character of world federalism, but we differ in the degree of emphasis laid on organizations like the North Atlantic Treaty Organization as compared to the United Nations. We are inclined to feel that the United Nations should be accepted and welcomed as a method of increasing the solidarity of the Free World but should not be permitted to deflect the policy of the United States in issues affecting national survival itself.

XII

GENERAL CONCLUSIONS

THE KEY to an understanding of the critical nature of foreign policy in our times is the conclusion reached in Chapter I: The conduct of foreign policy under conditions of national survival represents the struggle of what may be called a nation's "spirit" with its "fate."

The "spirit" of a nation is at once its heritage of cultural tradition and its concept of "the good life" for its own citizens and for the human race. Every nation tries to realize this more or less articulate pattern of concepts and habits in its own institutions and to spread by example, by precept, and sometimes by force the conditions which will create the same sort of ethical and institutional patterns in the world at large. It is not a matter of indifference to democracies which aim at freedom for humanity that other power systems should exist which aim at destroying freedom. History affords ample demonstration that the contest of the forces of the free spirit cannot be worked out within the boundaries of a single state any more than could the imposition of Marxian totalitarianism and planning for world conquest be successfully achieved within Russia alone. Today the two systems and all their intermediate variations determine the power balance of the world with peculiar force—now that the natural barriers to the spread of power in distance and strategic obstacles have dramatically lessened in importance with new weapons, including weapons of propaganda through modern communications. The Iron Curtain is the external face of any completely totalitarian system, necessary to protect itself from dangerous comparisons with free systems. The necessity for being always armed is the response of the democracies to the impact of the totalitarian pattern of aggression inherent in that system for its own survival and spread.

A nation's "fate" depends upon the circumstances of its own time in terms both of power and of challenge to the development of its way of life. The essence of great tragedy from the time of the Greeks has lain in the struggle of man's spirit with this surrounding web of destiny. The Greek city state did not meet the challenge. One culture after another has evolved through adjustments and sometimes catastrophic changes in the process of this struggle wherein new weapons, new tactics and military strategy, and the new dynamics of a compelling social myth, like that of the Moslems, have combined to try the issue of what type of civilization would spread to the limits of its possible span of control.

The United States in the nineteenth century naturally tended to forget this lesson, painfully stamped on history. We chose instead to rely on a combination of what might be called "oceanic security" and the growing hope that the enlightened peoples who controlled power might evolve conditions that would ban war and lead to an international organization strong enough to permit peaceful settlements on a live-and-let-live basis. The insight of the philosopher Kant in his *Toward Perpetual Peace* had shown, however, that the very conditions of such a live-and-let-live development for individuals and nations was a joining together for international control of "republican" (that is, constitutional) systems. To attempt a rule of law based upon moral community and common aims for national and individual development under freedom ruled out the possibility of founding such a union upon a federation of systems whose aims and ethos were basically hostile. The cleavage between totalitarian and free systems could not be bridged by any legerdemain of international organization erected on the formula of *union,* when no such *union* existed, either in aims or in methods.

Today's students of politics are increasingly aware of the basic importance of power, including physical force, to the nature of international relations and organization. They have become aware also, in smaller measure, that the great "social myths" which shape cultures determine the nature and use of this power. In short, it is not merely a matter of wealth or technical superiority that insures the health and survival of a civilization, but the belief in its values and their practice, even at heavy cost. Nowhere is this more clearly illustrated than in the great epics of historical cultures, which symbolize the life-drama of a civilization in the struggle of the legendary hero with surrounding forces and with trials put upon him by fate, typified in the primitive epics as "the gods." The Jewish, the Christian, the Greek epics, like the Roman, the Hindu, and Indo-European, have this strikingly common characteristic. The virtues people have sought to realize in their own lives through emulating the heroic virtues of a Heracles, a Moses, a Mohamet, have shaped civilizations. Today the struggle between the way of Lincoln and the way of Lenin is of the same order.

Foreign policy represents the continuous adjustment of a nation's drive toward the realization of its own values, both spiritual and material, with the corresponding drives of other nations, through a testing that does not stop short of war. We speak today of total war as if it were novel in human societies. But history throughout has shown only limited periods in which war did not fall far short of becoming total whenever a great clash of cultures, and what are today miscalled ideologies (for they might more simply and truly be called faiths), marked the nature of the times. The disappearance of empires, the ruthless extirpation of peoples or their transplanting elsewhere as slaves are not purely modern phenomena. After the Thirty Years War, the limited wars in the West were, on the whole, either dynastic or between peoples of cultural ideals so similar that survival of an entire people was not at issue. But this experience is perhaps not the norm of human history, even if it may well be the norm of war in what we would like to regard as a predominantly Christian civilization.

Our Christian civilization today, however, is confronted by a thoroughly non-Christian challenge, primarily and crucially by Moscow's crusading Marxism, but in smaller degree by the Islamic and nationalist movements newly risen in the Middle and the Far East. No one can doubt that the designs of Moscow do involve the imposition of a yoke of the most primitive type, comparable to the ruthlessness of Genghis Khan in his most destructive period, and going beyond the Great Khan in the effort to impose an ideology. The transplantation of whole populations is considered a normal feature of Politburo policy, whatever the cost of human life, to say nothing of the repression of every human right.

Confronted by this challenge, the United States of America has at once to hold to its own constitutional system and to show leadership in power politics for which it has had very little time (in terms of a nation's life) to develop the requisite responses. This requires strength, not only to endure, but to prevent. It is a role which our country has not had to play except at the time of its birth and, in more limited measure, during the Civil War period. The twentieth century brings it the new compulsion of two world wars with a third in prospect.

Our diplomats have been accustomed to living with dilemmas, but never before with dilemmas whose importance is of the magnitude of survival itself. The normal habit of diplomats in a period of quiet or in defense of the *status quo* is to nourish dilemmas, if not to cherish them. A dilemma becomes a professional challenge—"interesting," offering continuous fascination. A balance of power is subtly more attractive to them than an overbalance of power to enforce law. For great power systems on the march this is not the pattern. Diplomacy becomes a maneuver to undermine and weaken, in order more easily to crush. Its aggressive aim is to impose dilemmas on its prospective victims—to divide, to wear down, and to keep them on the defensive. Today it may not be enough for the free nations simply to gain time and avoid a showdown by striving to align power through the subtler means of propaganda and alliances in the diplomatic tradition—all in the pursuit of compromise and a new *modus vivendi*. American statesmanship must transcend this pattern and create at home and abroad a genuine center of power adequate to prevent war if possible, or to win it without catastrophic losses, if necessary.

The military, on the other hand, the other major component of our foreign policy, have traditionally been trained in a school too simple for the complex present. In the old school, abhorring dilemmas, they had no other remedy than to cut the Gordian knot. The soldier's role was only that of technical competence. Our military policy in the past could rely on the bulwarks of space and two great oceans, as well as on the tremendous reserve capacity of the American productive system, to make good any strategic and tactical errors, or even major political mistakes. Since their role was played down excessively in peace and played up excessively in war, and since they did not have the specialized and general staff training which characterized leading military systems abroad, their ability to carry real weight in political decisions and to contribute their own part in the power analyses necessarily was limited. Their intelligence systems were rudimentary, for lack both of appropriations and of their own imagination. The result has been a tendency for our policy-makers, without reliance on mature military skills, to lead the country first to underestimate the military component in formulating national policy, and then, in times of crisis, to yield uncritically to high policy decisions by military minds untrained in political grand strategy. This could and sometimes did compromise basic political issues.

The foreign policy of the United States has suffered in this way from the national habit of not taking the military seriously, and also from the consequence of an inadequate military participation in the making of foreign policy. On the record of the twentieth century, the military estimate of human nature and of power politics, even though oversimplified and often inadequate, might have been a better guide to our foreign policy than the sophistication (or naïveté) of the Department of State and our political leaders proved to be—if two world wars are the measure of failure. Had the pleas of our more mature military thinking been heeded, we should have had a defense force more adequate to back the foreign policy we assumed without a power base strong enough to support it. Perhaps Admiral Mahan kept us from national disaster by his emphasis on sea power in history, since even a Franklin D. Roosevelt, not otherwise too military minded, became a tenacious proponent and defendant of at least this arm of the nation's defensive strength. On the other hand, William Mitchell did not succeed in keeping us up to date in the matter of air supremacy; and it may be argued that military traditionalism itself was responsible for this miscarriage of national strategy. While there is a biting truth in Clemenceau's aphorism that war is too serious to be left to generals, it has also been observed that diplomacy may on occasion be too serious to be left to diplomats. One ought in justice to remember that failure to treat the generals *au sérieux* between wars produces the type of general to whom wars cannot be left. That this fault was deeply embedded in our whole culture and might be regarded as "historically" inevitable did not make it less a failure in national policy. Perhaps only "fate" can educate the "spirit" of the nation. But a nation's leaders also determine how rapidly that education may be acted upon.

A concomitant of underweighting the military in foreign policy has been exaggeration of the efficacy of the economic factor in foreign relations. In the twentieth century particularly this country has relied upon aid to other nations in the way of loans or Lend Lease or Economic Cooperation or technical assistance or UNRRA or the rebuilding of occupied territories to bolster up a shaky balance of power by building up man-power and military strength on the side of the democracies. Direct American military strength was regarded as a burden too expensive to be borne. Necessary as these economic pro-grams were, they should not have been considered, as they sometimes were, adequate substitutes for more positive policies and for the development of our own military strength where the latter implied heavy sacrifices in the United States itself. A telling example is the postwar budget in the United States, in which the military component had sunk to around 13 billion dollars by 1950, with a definite trend down toward 10 billion—and this in a period where the very survival of the nation itself was clearly at stake.

This disproportionate emphasis upon "economism"—measur-ing power merely in terms of total industrial production, gross national product and the like, instead of in weapons and trained manpower, or at the least that percentage of the national production that could be quickly and effectively diverted to war—was capable of leading to tragic error. So, too, was the assumption that a willingness to trade on our part would beget similar willingness to trade on the part of others and would produce an automatic prosperity adequate to check the ice floe of communist imperialism. These were the delusions of our time.

They were buttressed by mistaking moralizing for moral principles. This was a carryover from the era of Kellogg Pacts, of pinning hopes upon a World Court rather than upon real power sanctions, and upon a network of treaties without inquiry as to the ability and willingness of the other parties to keep them, or the power of our side to back them up. A corollary of this type of reasoning, shared even by some of the leaders of American opinion, was the Neutrality Act of the middle thirties, based on the childish assumption that merely controlling private arms manufacture and stopping trade with belligerents would put an end to war, or, at least, if applied rigorously by the United States alone, keep us out of this "nasty European habit" of fighting out power deadlocks, based on the clash of authoritarian and totalitarian with free systems.

These were in some measure the indices of immature national experience and the consequent immaturity of national opinion.

But there were also impressive elements of strength in our politics: the dynamics of the American system—its fundamental hold upon the basic strengths of freedom (including the education of its people) and the championing of national self-determination abroad (the basic premises of Wilson's much castigated policies); plus proven productive power, based on abundance of natural resources and on the qualities of improvisation inherent in free economies; plus, again, the capacity to get its citizens to work together as a team, in spite of clumsy administrative machinery—all these carried us through to military triumphs in two world wars. They did not, however, remove the causes of future conflicts, or prepare us better to prevent or meet them. Nor did they create either the overwhelming balance of power or the effective international organization which would have been needed to ease our burden.

Perhaps they could not have done so. Chief among the elements of tragedy is the inability of men to anticipate solutions for which their experience has not prepared them. Leadership itself feels these limits, and leadership, itself, is apt to lack both the imagination to conceive totally new solutions and the setting within which to elicit responses sufficient to carry them out. Yet American leadership during the twentieth century did point the way toward world organization, did create conditions of strength in the free world in two great wars, and is now seeking with some hope of success through organization and strength to prevent a third.

What mechanism has this leadership to work with and within? How are the responsibility of leadership and the response of opinion to be organized within our social and constitutional framework? These are the major issues requiring searching consideration. We point up these issues in order that others, we hope, may more adequately develop them.

OUR CONSTITUTIONAL SYSTEM:
STRENGTH AND LIMITATIONS

The form of government adopted in the American Constitution shows an eighteenth-century emphasis upon a mechanistic conception of checks and balances, culminating in the threefold separation of powers. This form endured because its organizational scheme fitted our basic theory of government. It reflected also the national effort to resolve a continuing double compulsion, which bears heavily on our problems in foreign policy today: Our "spirit" demanded, on the one hand, an attempt to establish the moral values of our constitutional system by emphasizing liberty and individual rights and the dynamics of freedom. On the other hand, there was, of necessity, the attempt to set up a government strong enough to unite the colonies for common defense and the general welfare. This required a powerful independent Executive and a federal union, in place of the weak confederacy, which had operated under a Congress that was little more than a council of ambassadors or a league of nations. The separation of powers, the checks and balances, the Bill of Rights, combined to spell out a distrust of unchecked power and to constitute an effort to prevent the rise of autocracy and a drift toward Caesarism. At the same time, the compulsion of survival demanded that the President be given control over at least the initiation of foreign policy, sweeping control over the armed forces and an independent tenure of office, subject to impeachment. Eventually the party system developed to give new meaning and flexibility to checks and balances. Party responsibility, even to the degree to which it has developed under our constitutional system, has tended to provide strong executive leadership capable in moments of crisis of breaking down the restrictions imposed by the separation of powers and operating under a "mandate" comparable to those granted in wartime.

In contrast, the British system went through a gradual transition from the royal prerogative to a powerful Cabinet representing the dominant party in the House of Commons, headed by a Prime Minister who could act independently of parliamentary control so long as the required majorities were forthcoming through party support. The device of calling a general election was intended in theory to secure the responsibility of the Cabinet to Parliament whenever an adverse vote in Parliament forced the issue of "no confidence"; but it gradually changed into a weapon for disciplining party majorities through the threat of dissolution. The British system has in practice, therefore, developed in the direction of a more thorough functional (as opposed to legal), separation of power than our own, since the executive is far more free from continuous legislative control. But if one looks behind appearances, this has been at the expense of subordinating the legislative body more and more to executive leadership and discipline, so that in fact the legislation itself is also the product of the executive. The House of Commons retains only a somewhat remote and ultimate type of control, either through threat of revolt against party discipline or in the event that no party commands a clear majority through a balancing party strength, such as that of the Liberals in the composition of the House. A defection of that balance from the support of the government could force a general election and therefore seriously affect policy decisions by the Cabinet.

Continental parliamentary systems have not enjoyed the strength of the American independent executive, because their legislative bodies have tended to hold the executive at their mercy by means of shifting combinations of multiple party support afforded by their electoral systems. Nor, on the other hand, have they possessed the unified and disciplined strength exercised by the British type of executive, who can rely upon the threat of a general election to force party discipline and assure a tighter control over the whole framework of policy.

All students recognize the strength of the British Foreign Office in foreign affairs, or, for that matter, of the Treasury in fiscal policy, especially when compared with the French or other parliamentary systems of the Continent. The same comparison holds against our own executive departments, if unification of policy and disciplined responsibility for a program are taken as the major criteria.

It would be unheard of in England, for example, to have a parliamentary inquest like that conducted by the Senate of the United States on the MacArthur removal, or by the House of Representatives on the Economic Cooperation Administration or on the Mutual Security Program. Hauling principal governmental officials, including civil servants, before parliamentary committees for castigation and almost unlimited inquiries into administrative proceedings and decisions—a normal proceeding in our own congressional hearings—is so contrary to the British parliamentary system that the spectacle is not afforded even in a country like Canada, whose ecomonic and social systems and federal organization in other respects closely parallel our own. Under the parliamentary system, the Cabinet interposes the shield of collective responsibility. Reversed, this can require disciplined support from parliament and can limit inquiries only to broad lines of policy. This is nowhere better illustrated than in the budget, which is susceptible of no significant amendment in the British system; whereas a budget in the United States suffers a fate only less drastic than (to paraphrase John Hay) a treaty sometimes suffers in going before the Senate: "It is like a bull entering the ring—extremely unlikely to emerge alive." One might add, "Or if alive, unmutilated." The President, who has called for ten billion more in new taxation, has to take half a loaf.

This comparison has often led those who long for a more logically integrated and better controlled foreign policy to yearn for the British parliamentary system and to raise questions as to how our own might be given similar advantages. There are, however, offsetting considerations in the American system. Foreign policies, to cite a prime example, are more dramatically debated; thus there is a better chance of developing a deeper basis of public support when successful integration is possible. Those who would urge the advantages of having Congress share more actively, as well as critically, in the making of foreign policy point out that such public support is now more essential than ever, since foreign policy is geared into every aspect of the nation's political and economic life. Taking the federal budget as a rough measure of the comparative importance of foreign policy in the whole of our national life, it is sufficient to note that foreign policy in its broadest sense (including defense and foreign economic aid in all its forms) at present accounts for at least three quarters of federal expenditures; and the percentage is steadily rising. Furthermore foreign affairs extends throughout the entire range of governmental agencies. This poses problems of integration at the presidential level, as well as of gaining support of the many committees of Congress other than those dealing primarily with foreign affairs.

The "grand inquest" technique used in congressional hearings and debates, the clash of interest groups and propaganda support, the efforts of foreign governments to influence American opinion at all levels—all call for a degree of sophistication in the electorate which, it is argued, can only be produced by the perpetual processes of education involved in the normal conflicts produced by a separation of powers. In short, according to this reasoning, the testing of policies today is not simply one of private arrangements within the diplomatic corps of a foreign office, but one wherein the support of public opinion on an overwhelming basis is a necessity.

Bipartisanship is the expression of the hope and necessity of transcending mere party responsibility when national survival itself may be at stake. Proponents of the American system argue that bipartisanship is at least as possible under our loose party discipline as it is under the British parliamentary system, where bipartisanship and governments of national union or of coalitions of parties have served in times of great stress.

In dealing with the limitations imposed by the separation of powers upon responsible integration of foreign policy, both in its formation and in its execution, the following crucial questions, noted before, bear repeating here in succinct but less developed form:

Does the separation of powers produce a better education of opinion and, as a result, a more unifying force for the adoption and support of foreign policies?

Is party discipline sufficiently possible in the American system to prevent shifting coalitions of congressional support on issues that may destroy the integrity of a foreign policy, that is, its inner consistency in terms of a genuine strategy?

Can the separation of powers produce or permit a broad enough common policy to insure the continuity in foreign policy on which other nations must be able to depend? Or, does it produce a minimum kind of stability of authority otherwise difficult to provide in a democratic republic?

Does it permit or encourage the kind of foresight in anticipating, if need be with sacrifices adequate to future probabilities, the type of preparation in terms of strength, military and economic, essential for leadership by the United States in the free world? Is it able to secure our national survival?

The case for the separation of powers as an educational device has to some degree been explored above. The case rests ultimately upon the assumption that dramatizing issues through congressional debates and hearings is the best method of educating opinion to the necessities of foreign policy. Essentially this view rests upon the idea that out of conflicts will emerge unity and that a fruitful resolution is the natural resultant of the conflict of pressures.

This optimistic view of the mechanics of force involved in pressure politics requires evaluation. The channeling of drives and interests to a common end and a common democratic response to fundamental issues is possible if there is a sufficient cultural homogeneity in the population, a community of tradition, and, above all, a sufficient crudity in the forms of external attack to strike home at the most elementary levels, as well as enough *time* for us to react even with the slow processes we must follow.

Fortunately we have had these advantages in the past when foreign autocracies have challenged the United States. The setting has been consistently one of extremely crude shocks by the opposing systems, by the Axis before and during World War II and by Moscow's behavior since then. Our responses have been those of a nation reasonably sophisticated in the analysis of propaganda efforts, internal and external, and reasonably united in support of the broader ranges of both economic and political objectives. We have been kicked into unity, and kicking fortunately has been the habit of our opponents. The kicks were light, not aimed to kill.

Moreover, through a combination of factors no longer present, we were blessed in the past by having plenty of time to make the necessary adjustments before survival became a real issue. More than that, we have had enough economic power to offset diplomatic blunders and lack of integrated policies.

On the other side, however, we must take into account the necessity which Presidents have felt to carry along an almost overwhelming support of public opinion before they would act. This has meant an inability or unwillingness to act against a 25 or 30 percent opposition of such strenuous character as to endanger success at the polls. It is not merely a question of one third of the Senate blocking treaties, as was the case with President Wilson and the League; but also of the need for placating groups, which, for example, demand neutrality legislation or advocate to the last ditch a virulent type of isolationism, strongly enough organized to throw their weight between parties or to dominate a party. Note, for example, how Franklin D. Roosevelt soft-pedaled the "Quarantine" idea after his challenging speech in 1937.

Could great "leadership" under our system have forced a more active policy to restrain the outbreak of either World War I or World War II? Was the drag on policy due more to a general democratic unwillingness to forecast the future and undertake necessary sacrifices in time? Or was the result peculiarly shaped by the way in which the separation of powers magnifies the effectiveness of pressure politics in the United States? The answers to these questions may well demand a more penetrating and deeper insight through political and historical analysis than has yet been brought to bear. It is a prime challenge to our most mature thinking.

The answer to the question of the adequacy of party control *to assure coherence in foreign policy* depends in considerable measure upon whether the mechanics of the American system inherently impose peculiar limitations on party discipline and responsibility. Opinions naturally differ as to degree, but the weight of high-level political thinking today concedes that well-organized minority pressures have excessive weight in our system. This has particularly harmful effects on the nation's success in controlling all policy, and controlling foreign policy in particular. The difficulty with "free" combinations of congressional support in both Houses is that on a particular issue, *without strict party discipline,* particular pressures may lead a Congressman to support a measure that destroys the integrity of a whole system of foreign policy. Hurried congressional debate in the limited period of consideration which can be afforded to even the most important legislation may not always bring out the critical character of a single measure in an Administration program. Just as a meat price "rollback" may precipitate an adverse congressional vote that can undo a whole system of price controls, so cutting out aid in some particular segment vital to the whole program of foreign assistance or enforcing the will of Congress in a manner calculated to destroy the necessary cooperation of other countries, could, without adequate understanding of the fact, knock out the underpinnings of a whole integrated foreign relations program. *This is the nub of the case for party discipline as essential to reliable control and assured coherence in foreign policy.* The strength of the British system is that it can marshal support at need *on any issue.* In comparison, the operation of the American system is terribly chancy, as in the instance where the whole draft legislation and selective service were saved by only one vote in the House a few months before Pearl Harbor.

It may be argued that this kind of fumble on chance issues can generally be corrected in time. But the crucial nature of timing in modern circumstances may not always give the opportunity for correction. The congressional claim to their own interpretations or assessments of intelligence as to the objectives and moves of foreign countries exposes presidential policy to a perpetual gantlet, where a chance blow by one of the tomahawks may kill a policy that it was only intended to mark or mutilate slightly. Senator Borah's pride in the superiority of his sources of political intelligence was typical of the amateur experts in foreign policy who passed the neutrality legislation in 1937. Today our leaders in Congress are generally less sure of their sources, but the danger exists. How is its importance to be weighed? What are the remedies?

The same considerations underlie the question of *continuity of policy*. A program or policy involves both inner coherence, as considered under the previous question, and the guarantee of a duration long enough really to test its possibilities. During the heyday of British foreign policy, when the views of His Majesty's government could be forecast with considerable certainty in spite of changes of the party in power in the United Kingdom, and when Britain's sea power and economic and imperial strength lent commanding stability to the European concert of powers, the world enjoyed a remarkable period of peaceful expansion and of the development of human rights. The need for a similarly responsible opposition, ready and able to share sufficiently in the making of current policy to continue the same broad outlines under a change of administration, may be of critical importance to the future of leadership by the United States in the free world. Without such continuity, other nations are exposed to the necessity of "hedging" their support of United States policies or to the need of insuring themselves by adopting separate lines of policy against the "incalculable" possibilities of radical changes in Washington.

This charge was the one most frequently leveled at the United States after the defeat of Wilson's proposal to join the

League of Nations. Today a sweeping victory for the isolationist or at least the "non-cooperationist" wing of the Republican party in 1952, for example, might possibly produce basic realignments of the policies of many European countries.

We do not suggest that foreign policy is "good" to the degree that it never alters. Foreign policy, by its very nature, must not only adjust with great rapidity to altered circumstances but must also be capable of correcting past errors. In that sense it is and must be perpetually "revisionist." On the other hand, the mechanism of its formation should afford a reasonable opportunity to make the revision in a continuous way, rather than by an abrupt *volte face*, as the result of a single election. This tends to emphasize once more the necessity for responsible opposition and for disciplined support on a bipartisan basis, but with a working majority under strong party discipline.

Aside from continuity of policy, can continuity and stability of executive authority—which become more important in times of crisis—be assured in a democratic republic by any other constitutional form than our present separation of powers, or be better assured?

The real question that confronts those concerned about the adequacy of American foreign policy today and the instruments through which it must be formulated and controlled is not its past successes or failures but its *ability to meet present and future challenges*. Past experience may be a useful guide to the possibilities of the present. But the test ahead is crucial.

From what has gone before, it may be concluded that the strength of our system lies in its ability to mobilize massive support when unmistakably confronted by external threat or after the event, for example, after a Pearl Harbor. Its strength is also to be found in a quite unusual degree of national unity on policies which, even in a period of legal "peace," have time to be developed slowly under the pressure of external challenges and the logic of events. In spite of the difficulties imposed by the sharing of powers, as much as by their separation, *the formation of our foreign policy has shown a willingness of the people to take on economic burdens through foreign assistance and to respond in times of absolute crisis with vigor and determination and with a great degree of national unity.*

On the other hand, *the lack of integrated party responsibility,* comparable to that possible in the British Parliamentary system, *has certainly increased the effectiveness of pressure and propaganda groups in delaying action, or increasing timidity or confusion in programs.* There is no more dramatic example than the fact, noted above, that when, prior to Korea, the military budget of this country had fallen to almost 13 billion dollars and was programmed down to 10 billions, the President further lopped about three quarters of a billion from the authorized annual appropriations for the Air Force, even after that sum had actually been appropriated by Congress. Political pressures for "economy" on the one side and for the Welfare State on the other combined to make this possible. It should be noted in fairness that Britain had been led by Baldwin and Chamberlain to an almost similar state of unpreparedness prior to Munich, when the Labour Party was a very ineffectual opposition and the temper of Britain supported Chamberlain's policy rather than that of Churchill. Is this a general weakess of democracy? Is it increased by a system that weakens executive leadership?

The nature of foreign policies obviously cannot be treated simply as a function of any mechanical arrangement of political machinery. *Still it may be agreed that all those factors which multiply delay and make conciliation of strongly organized pressure groups necessary do handicap longer-term planning and the acceptance of the necessary sacrifices that foresight in planning entails.* The recent struggle over price and wage controls, at one time even threatening the continuance of the basic authorizations by Congress for the defense program, was the product of numerous pressures against which there appeared to be no effective way of forcing and dramatizing the national interest, even though the country seemed very largely, but passively, aligned in favor of stabilization.

The shortest summary statement of this difficulty is that strong pressure groups and minority interests, operating from different political bases but to the common end of frustration, are more likely where the Executive lacks effective measures for party discipline and for mobilizing support that will count in legislative elections. Are his ways of appealing for political support on national issues adequate? The way in which Congressmen get elected is certainly pretty decisive on their voting habits. This dependence on local issues in elections does not strengthen national policy. Such a system impels the Executive toward either a masterly indirection, or a positive timidity in facing difficult issues, certainly in forcing their solution. Some critics have thought to find in our Far Eastern policy in particular a reflection of the latter. Even where the President has assumed a strongly determined attitude, he has not always presented it by a method effective enough to win the requisite popular support and to influence Congress.* The resulting compromise has been costly, remains dangerous, and can at best gain only time and keep this country armed and anxious. Perhaps either alternative might have been better than the compromise. Or was the compromise more wise because it forced a middle path between extremes?

Here again we point to problems and their setting that demand more systematic and deeper study for answers.

* The State Department had so lost its nerve under the McCarthy attacks that at one point a spokesman denied ever having had the recognition of Communist China under consideration—palpably untrue, and grossly negligent of the alternatives of policy had it been true.

ASSUMPTIONS AS TO THE NATURE
OF THE THREAT AND ITS TIMING

From our discussions have come certain convictions and more questions about the relation of political process and machinery to the total historical setting within which a foreign policy is framed. This changed emphasis is reflected more or less unconsciously in the change of tone one may note as between periods of distinctly different character in this country—for example, the post-Civil War and Wilsonian periods, or that of American naïveté in the twenties and thirties, as compared with the trend toward Machiavellian analysis or emphasis solely upon power politics currently becoming fashionable. In a broad sense, not only the substantive policies but the machinery necessary to realize them depend on the higher reaches of political analysis, including the setting of national strategy. The choice of alternatives, the degree to which a bold and well-integrated solution is to be preferred to patchwork, the capacity of a democracy to adjust to new challenges and to discover methods of effective action, *means* to *ends*—all depend upon the degree of recognition of a threat to its existence and to its future. Two world wars have been fought in which our policy emphasized the need for creating a "world safe for democracy," on a basis of national self-determination through free elections, coupled with the League of Nations or a United Nations organized in hope of a world rule of law and the punishment of aggression. The search not only for national but for international machinery capable of coping with the problem was never more clearly high-lighted than in the struggle within the United Nations to secure an agreed and enforceable formula for control, on an international basis, for atomic energy and atomic weapons.

People led to believe that the destruction of the Nazi tyranny would produce a brave new world or, at a secondary level, that the United Nations contained as if by formula some special magic for peace, tended in the face of world events to fall into disillusionment and reaction. In the first place, they felt that since the objectives they were told they were fighting for had been fulfilled, demobilization was in order as speedily as possible and the resumption of a peace footing was not only safe but good sense. When that proved to have been based on a miscalculation, they fell back on the extremes of either pacifism or straight power politics, demanding impossible remedies. On the one hand, the pacifists advocate policies which could hold hope only if there were Quakers also in the Politburo. On the other hand, there are those who would welcome Caesarism as a relief from the struggle to understand and guide responsible government in so complicated a world.

It has not been our intention to assess the substantive merits of our foreign policy or to presume to suggest a sweeping solution of all our problems through some new orientation. But, with some divergences in terms of the application of the principles to policies, we are agreed that underlying assumptions as to the nature of our system, its responses and possibilities in forming effective foreign policy, are colored by the degree to which those who ultimately make policy can correctly gauge the seriousness and the nature of the contemporary challenge. It is obvious from past experience that preoccupation with an immediate task, such as winning a war against one enemy, may, in the very nature of democratic propaganda and morale-building, tend to obscure quite as basic threats that have a longer-run significance. To estimate how really survival is at stake and what factors affect survival —indeed, *what it is that we are trying to make sure will survive* —must constitute the all-important framework on which policy must be formed. Can our present methods of assessing these problems furnish the best guidance for this nation at this time?

The seriousness of these problems and the nature of their remedies can be estimated only in the light of one's assumptions about the probable behavior of the Politburo. On the one hand, some argue that the glacial aspect of Moscow's imperialism precludes bold risks or direct aggression like that of the Nazis and proceeds by a series of carefully calculated pressures and "feeling out" actions. Those who believe in the policy of "containment, but not too much," urge that too great a show of determination on our part to advance our ideas of a free world and to build adequate force to that end might create the conviction in Moscow that we meant war, and that this itself might precipitate war. On this assessment of the psychology of the Kremlin, our very failures to take decisive action and our willingness to continue an indefinite series of compromises and delaying actions may avoid a showdown by encouraging Moscow to rely upon the Marxist faith that the system of free government and economics (of which we are the power leader) must inevitably disintegrate. Therefore, this line holds, Moscow believes that the fulfillment of fixed objectives will not require war. Furthermore, Russians don't attack first. They are not gamblers like Hitler. Alternatively, according to this reasoning, our preparations may at some future date, say, by 1954, have reached such a state as to deter war by making it too costly and too risky for Moscow.

The alternative assumption, baldly stated, rests upon the inevitability of war, unless (*and this is held to be a very improbable* "unless") the Russian system should itself disintegrate (perhaps after Stalin's death) and lose its hold on its well-disciplined puppets abroad. This analysis rests partly upon the crusading nature of communism as a world challenge, but even more on the conviction that the Russian system cannot survive if free and flourishing systems can and do exist as great power bases capable of challenging not only the military supremacy of the communist camp but its hold on the imagination and hopes of its own people and of those whom it has enslaved elsewhere. Under this pressure of comparison, the iron curtain is not enough. Moscow must destroy freedom abroad to avoid being undermined by the desire for freedom at home. Therefore it cannot change its pattern of aggressive imperialism.

A further assumption, however, must be considered in the light of both these hypotheses. The "containment and deterrent" school of thought operates clearly on the assumption that "time is on our side" and that an endurable measure of preparation shared by free nations will produce a power balance so overwhelmingly against Moscow as to force its "realistic" abandonment of imperialistic designs, or to force the regime to crack up through its own internal strains. If time is on our side, then delay and conciliation and even some measure of appeasement may be worth the risk, since that would be calculated to give us the precious years needed for rebuilding Germany and Japan and for strengthening the bonds of the free world.

The other school ("inevitability of war") must also answer the question "Is time on our side?" in order to formulate the alternatives of its future policy. If Russian atomic strength increases to a point where a surprise attack might be possible, the prognostic would be, quite understandably, that *time may not be on our side,* and our system of delayed responses may invite tragedy. Moreover the vulnerability of our harbors, the possible prevention by the Soviet defense of air attacks by weapons like our B-36, the improvement of the proximity fuse, electronics, guided missiles against aircraft or with atomic warheads, the increase of the effectiveness of jet interceptor and radar devices—these and other factors might render our weapons increasingly less effective and the Russian weapons increasingly more effective. In addition, Europe might be cut off from effective support by a combination of schnorkel submarines and the mining or atomic destruction of our own harbors and sea lanes as well as theirs. Then time would definitely not be on our side, since we would become increasingly vulnerable to a devastating surprise attack; the Soviets, less.

This latter assumption would have justified taking such risks in 1950 as Generals MacArthur and Wedemeyer had recommended and would certainly justify a much bolder past and present policy than has been thought to be possible by even the Joint Chiefs of Staff. Its rejection indicates the adoption of a policy along the lines the Administration is following, with a patient build-up of strength, putting trust in the winning to the West of Germany and Japan and a gradual elimination of the threat of communist parties to the stability and defense potential of the Western nations of Europe particularly. The military assessment must also measure our own growth in capabilities for the use of the "fantastic weapons," just about to be possible on a mass scale, according to press reports. Our whole mobilization program, its magnitude and timing, is geared to the assumption that strength can be achieved within a year or two sufficient to be a deterrent to war and a block to Moscow's imperialistic objectives.

Yet alternatives are never quite so clear even as these in the realm of political probabilities. This is the dilemma of those who must guide policy. Even if a choice of basic attitude is made, new factors may arise which will force considerable readjustments. The Korean episode, for example, has tended to stiffen the hitherto less militarily strong position of the Administration and to speed up a policy of really leading the free world, and leading it from strength. Our policies in the Far East notably stiffened, also. Policy-framers must also weigh the quite real possibility that democracies may find it difficult to maintain continuous pressure over a long time and, from sheer weariness of tension, be particularly vulnerable to the blandishments of peace offensives and to hope for so-called "settlements." There is, on the other hand, also a possibility that tension may breed increased impatience and a desire for a showdown.

How much is the political system itself a shaper of decisions along these lines? The recent inquest on the whole basis of our strategy and foreign policy in congressional hearings on the MacArthur dismissal and the Mutual Security Assistance program did not succeed in throwing very much more light on these basic issues. Though our grand strategy, even in some detail, was exposed to the view of friend and enemy alike so far as the more obvious outlines were concerned, much of the really critical material was necessarily secret and "off the record" for public consumption. Conceivably it was not presented in its entirety even to Congress.

The "fantastic weapons" were not unveiled in any outline for many months after the MacArthur inquiry and still remain matters of mystery to most people, in spite of official revelations in the press (recently deplored by Mr. Truman) as to the development of guided missiles and atomic weapons. Most important of all, the potentialities of the *Russian* system in similar matters are among the most closely guarded of military secrets. Moreover it has been asserted that it is a well-defined policy of the Defense Department not to divulge some of its policies, as well as its top intelligence, particularly in formative stages, to the decision-making agencies on the civilian side of the government, even to the top-level National Security Council. This is probably an exaggerated claim, but there is undoubtedly a natural reluctance on the part of military authorities to open up their plans to the prying eyes of civilians. This is based not only on dangers to "security" in the sense of secrecy, but upon a desire to escape civilian interference and to control even the scheduling and character of mobilization from the vantage point of a military estimate of the total situation. The inability of Congress to grapple with defense budgets in any technical detail is paralleled to a degree by the inability of civilian agencies concerned with mobilization to control military service programming, particularly contracts and military scheduling of end items by any measures except by withholding credits or materials. Certain aspects of diplomacy involve the same problems of secrecy.*

This raises in very trenchant form the dilemma of democracy. Unless it is capable of acting with foresight and compelling control of national policy well in advance of crisis, it may prove entirely ineffectual to meet the kind of challenge which a ruthless totalitarian system presents—if that system can command anything like equal strength, plus surprise.

Yet, it is argued by those who fear the other horn of the dilemma, delegation of powers to a temporary dictator may lose for us our democratic character almost as effectually as if the country had been defeated in war; though conceivably any dictatorship of our own would be more palatable than that of a foreign enemy.

On balance, the challenge of the times would appear to indicate, that, *at a minimum*, the Executive's hands should be strengthened to such a degree that he is able to form a program under a political mandate given in advance and with the assurance of continued popular support for a period of years. There is no guarantee that even the tighter and more disciplined response of the British system would automatically achieve this end; though conceivably it would function very differently in a power situation like our own than in an ex-

---

* Admittedly, Congress does not always act on information available to it. On the other hand, recent security action like that taken by the President through an executive order to tighten up security measures and classification of official papers may, even when entirely necessary to cut down dangerous security leaks, have a serious tendency to make public judgment and informed congressional action still more difficult.

hausted and receding empire. The crucial issue seen by those who realistically confront the challenge of American foreign policy is how to achieve greater strengthening of the Executive and greater wisdom of leadership, while avoiding Caesarism and the loss of civil liberties that protect real freedom. There is, after all, no guarantee that Caesarism will produce either the wise leadership or the national unity which is implied or hoped by resort to this desperate remedy. Rather the lessons of history, so far as we are able to discern them, indicate that the decline of a democracy is not more certain than the destruction of an empire. The fate which this nation's spirit must confront and master requires an *epic leadership, within the democratic tradition.*

We are convinced that no formula is available to assure the automatic success of a democracy in confronting the kind of world in which we now live. We recognize with encouragement, with hope, the progress that has been made in educating American opinion to responsibilities of world leadership in a few brief decades. We recognize also the inherent difficulties of maintaining party controls and responsibility and, at the same time, of transcending partisanship in foreign policy. The energy and devotion with which a large number of voluntary groups participate in this effort cannot guarantee that out of the welter of conflict and public examination will come strong action where it is required, or unified support at the right time and on the right issues. Who, after all, can be absolutely certain, with more than human wisdom, of what are the *right* solutions and the *right* timing? Yet we must act responsibly on the best light we have: "with firmness in the right, as God gives us to see the right," said Lincoln.

We hope that we have pointed to the right problems and to the alternatives in assumptions and methods of organizing better control involved in our foreign policy: Others may be aided to reach better solutions than we have so far achieved as a nation through the challenge of our analysis to further and deeper insights.

ISSUES FOR RESEARCH

This necessarily limited summary of our major conclusions and some of the open issues that remain suggest the real fruitfulness of the inquiry:

Basically the major importance of this study is its emphasis on the misdirected attention of American scholarship and of American public opinion. There can be little quarrel with the range, volume, and technical adequacy of the *descriptive* studies on the American system. If one compares the outpouring of books and articles of every kind on the operation of our own system with the real paucity of any such material on the European systems, even on the British, one might be inclined to become self-congratulatory, if not complacent, in terms of sheer energy and amount of research.

But is not the object of research *understanding?*

It is in this light that contemporary studies of American foreign policy, even in its formulation and control aspects, seem most inadequate. *To get the right answers, one must first of all ask the right questions.* Has the level of analysis in the American system been characterized by understanding *in depth?* Do we not need to examine our *basic assumptions* more thoroughly, in order to avoid waste effort and to meet the seriousness of our challenge?

Schools of cultural determinism—or, for that matter, of other forms of determinism—and efforts to "quantify" solutions of problems have proved almost useless in posing inquiries into the basic assumptions that should govern all inquiries into the nature of foreign policy, as we have considered it here. On the one hand, unless study of social relations and cultures is aimed at strengthening the capacity to choose between alternatives and to surmount what at the beginning we spoke of as the "nation's fate," it can only serve to undermine in the deepest way the *morale* of a civilization by generating a fundamental pessimism as to its possibilities of action. One may object that an exception can be made for types of determinism, like Marxism, which predict inevitable victory through the historical process itself. But the shallowness of this analysis in terms of any philosophical perspective becomes obvious when its inner contradictions are examined. Some myths are of no use to a democracy. Our beliefs must stand rational analysis.

As a myth, such formulations may serve the same ends that the Fascist and the Nazi myths served, if they are indoctrinated by totalitarian methods. But "scientism" is of little value for our free systems as applied to the study of human relations and politics in its broadest sense, in so far as it is based on assumptions which govern inquiries into physical nature. Patterns of culture are useful in examining the *limits* of a civilization, not its *possibilities*. Men are not mere chemical elements in some sort of controlled test tube. Nothing but misunderstanding comes from treating them as if they were so.

When the tool of "quantification"—that is, the reduction of human behavior to measurable and predictable reactions—is applied, all the failings of pseudo-science emerge. That there are determined elements in any equation affecting human behavior (for example, physical resources, population growth over a narrow time span, the level of technology, and sun spots) there can be no question. But the effects of these are susceptible to rearrangement. It is well to keep in mind that it was not the technology of the Arab world which assured the triumph of the Moslems. Rather it was the ability of the aroused and crusading Moslems to adopt, adapt, and control techniques and to apply them to the ends of Islam.

A summary example may be useful: the power *potential* of

the Western world outside the control of Moscow is at this reading at least treble and in many cases quadruple or quintuple the potentialities available to Moscow. But the inner dynamics of Western civilization, the organization of its resources and the ability to turn potential power into effective military force, present quite another face. How much potential can be made available for the period of decision? Unless the West finds not only its organizing idea but its spiritual unity and its determination *in terms of creating a future* for Europe and for other peoples now on the march toward new goals, the mobilization of resources *in time* is a matter of doubt, at best. Sacrifice, freely accepted, must match the imposed sacrifices which have built up Moscow's present lead in actually available striking forces of many types.

FOCAL POINTS FOR EMPHASIS

For purposes of pointing up the neglected issues into which the Woodrow Wilson Foundation might encourage deeper inquiry, the Introduction has already indicated our primary emphasis. We pointed out there that the *presuppositions of any foreign policy depend upon assumptions as to the nature of human nature.* Human nature in its relation to politics is the foundation for any inquiry into political organization and processes. We are equally convinced that a meaningful study of politics, especially crucial to the field of foreign policy, must include searching inquiry into such key problems as the nature of power, the idea of national interest, the relation of these to basic human values, such as the dignity of human personality and the relation of man to the total universe in which he lives. *Such a study would underlie questions as to the nature and the use of the mechanics of our system,* the relation of these mechanics to our national survival in terms of events which may challenge our ability to preserve and recreate the spiritual values which are the heritage of our civilization.

It is in this light that the *ends of foreign policy as stated in the Introduction seem to us matters which contemporary scholarship has least successfully handled.* There have been any number of descriptive and piecemeal approaches, but few bold attempts to formulate at deeper levels the problems that we raised in the Introduction and which we feel should be highlighted for future analysis. The main point of our preliminary inquiry is to point up the importance of these neglected areas.

The true nature of "intelligence," its assessment and use, underlie most of the policy issues involved. Its study is therefore central. *"Intelligence" extends not only to adequate collection of information by every channel, but its evaluation for policy formulation and purposeful action.*

Without decrying or writing down the need for descriptive studies, we must conclude that these are of use only when related to a sophisticated set of assumptions relevant to actual experience and to existing institutional devices. For that reason we revert to the schema laid out in the Introduction for the analysis of foreign policy under broad topics where research activities (in the truer sense of the term) of American scholars and of practitioners might be appropriately channeled. Appendix I aims at making somewhat more detailed suggestions within this frame.

A historically inaccurate but very descriptive phrase of American attitude was once made: "Millions for defense, but not one cent for tribute." This entirely worthy and right attitude was intended to characterize a firm attachment to a moral principle without which, in the judgment of the men of that time, a nation could not survive or maintain its own self respect.

A foreign policy that forgets the distinction between "tribute" and "defense" is in danger. To prevent such a misconception, it is equally important that the scholars of a nation should not adopt a formula: "Millions for description but not one cent for true insight" (what we have called *understanding*). The Woodrow Wilson Foundation seems to us a peculiarly appropriate agency for reminding this nation of the need, indeed the necessity, for really fundamental analyses of the presuppositions on which all foreign policy and the methods of its control must rest. "By their fruits, ye shall know them."

APPENDICES

I: FUTURE RESEARCH

THE CONTINUING CRISIS in world affairs forces American scholarship to face up to a difficult question: do we know how to organize the government of the United States for the conduct of its foreign policy and for the role that it must play in the organization of the United Nations?

By formal amendment and informal development, the American system of government is continually altered to meet new needs. In a very real sense, the work of 1787 will never be finished; the American people, by ceaselessly adapting their political institutions to meet the challenge of current affairs, are in a continuous constitutional convention.

How well they will meet the present challenge will depend in the long run on the way in which they and their leaders understand the nature of their governmental system, and its relation to the forces and ideas that have convulsed the twentieth-century world. For about a century, American statesmen and scholars alike were spared the necessity of facing up to some of the fundamental problems of human society that are grounded in the struggle for power and survival among nations. But now the threat of communism makes us think again about issues that have not been critical in the western world since the wars of religion subsided; the atomic bomb raises problems that the English-speaking nations thought they had solved forever by adopting bills of rights and by putting armies under civilian control.

Statesmen and citizens generally can hardly be expected to deal with these issues before scholars have even recognized their existence. The great opportunity of scholars and research workers today is to help the American people to see how directly some of the fundamental principles of human freedom depend on our ability to deal with the immediate practical problems of organizing the government of the United States for the conduct of ˙its foreign affairs. They can rise to this opportunity if they are willing to comprehend the whole range of constitutional and political and administrative issues involved, and if they understand that the most practical of these issues are related directly to some of the age-old problems of human nature and human society.

Can men be free to shape the form of their social institutions —to constitute their governments by deliberate action to serve the purposes of peace and law? Or are men fundamentally at the mercy of blind psychological or economic forces? Can the men who hold great power in society, by their command of military force or scientific knowledge, be made responsible in some effective way to a rule of law and to all the people, or does society depend on some sort of trained elite to control its development? Such questions as these are as old as history, but every age must ask them anew, and try to answer them in a way that will control the development of its institutions.

In this study we have tried to see how these basic questions are related in practical ways to the current crisis in world affairs, and to the current threat to our national security and freedom. Its observations and suggested reforms were made throughout the several topics treated not in any spirit of dogmatic finality, but in order to put forward for study and action a closely connected series of problems that must be solved if the United States is to improve the organization of its government for the conduct of foreign affairs. This only begins the job. How can it be taken up, and pushed ahead, to provide public officers and private citizens with the most intelligent basis of action possible?

It may be helpful to outline some of the most important areas or topics that we considered worthy of systematic study. But first it may be well to comment briefly on the way in which research is done—the problem of the research method.

METHODS OF RESEARCH

Methodology, which is the aspect of research most forbidding to the layman, is only the business of knowing how to ask the right questions, and to pursue the right inquiries, in order to find out something that is important.

Some scholarly methodology, of course, looks very much like an elaborate Rube Goldberg apparatus that grinds out a comparatively useless product. It is easy to make so much of problems of method that one never get results—like packing endlessly for a journey on which one never starts. Nevertheless, the very statement of any problem implies a method, as does the choice of facts or data that one wishes to examine. How you select certain facts rather than others, choose some to emphasize, and ultimately interpret their significance in theory and practice—all this is a question of research method.

In dealing with the subjects which we have discussed it is especially difficult to know how much to make use of the "scientific method," in the sense in which that term is used both in the physical sciences and in such social sciences as psychology and sociology. Certainly the experimental method and the techniques of measurement and statistical proof cannot be applied to all aspects of broad political and constitutional issues.

Many factors in international affairs are capable of scientific measurement. The statistical method, for example, is indispensable for the study of the logistics of raw materials, or of industrial productive capacity. But what scientific method can deal with the possibility that a new social myth will arise that will transform a whole society? A Marx or a Mahomet, a Buddha or a Christ may change the whole system of limitations that determine the strength of human societies.

Material inventions, themselves the product of human thought and values, by the development of new weapons have upset the advance calculations of power. Great strategists have done unexpected things with the limited means at their disposal. But—more important—the conviction of a "mission" and of inevitable victory may determine the destiny of a civilization.

It is both theoretically possible, and extremely useful for political and administrative purposes, to measure various aspects of morale, and various attitudes that make up morale. But in another sense, and perhaps a deeper one, to measure morale is to kill it. No matter how finely you dissever the living reality with your learned knife, it is never the reality that you have when you have finished, for you have killed it in the operation; one may put the matter thus, roughly paraphrasing an idea from Dostoevski.

Similarly, while a study like economics may establish patterns of behavior that are useful guides within its own assumptions, and within a given social or cultural setting, the great decisions as to its uses are political decisions and, in the last analysis, moral decisions. Even Marx recognized this when he made his system turn on the *methods of control*—by men, and for freedom—*over* the instruments of production. A more thorough materialism would have assumed that the means of production themselves would have determined the methods of control. Marxism is thus fundamentally muddled as to its basic premise: materialistic (economic) determinism of the historical process.

But all this does not reduce the role of a genuinely scientific method; indeed, it increases it in scope and variety. The biological as well as the social sciences may tell us much about what men and nations can do and cannot do, and how their potentialities may be increased. They have much to contribute to the study of the nature of man, which must underlie our approach to national and international politics. They may enrich our understanding of social institutions, including the practical fields of administration and management, as well as the broader aspects of social relations and political institutions.

How much the social sciences as a whole may contribute will depend not only on their several specific techniques, but on the way in which they are interpreted and applied. The greatest lack of fruitfulness of most research in the humanities, the social sciences, law and history, and perhaps even in the natural sciences, comes from the lack of broad interpretation. This is no more true of statistical and quantitative research than of the descriptive and historical studies that make up the greater part of research in political science today. These studies are likely to fall into one of two opposite traps—either to be so loftily detached, with the color of objectivity, that they irresponsibly ignore the difficulties and problems of the practical administrator or politician; or, on the other hand, to espouse some reform so warmly that they distort their facts to prove a point. They may share the weakness of some of the supposedly "scientific" studies, which isolate a specialty from its context so completely that it loses all reality. Or they may neglect entirely the dynamic of values and the role played by humanly developed ethical norms.

In a field as complex in its historical roots and its living development as foreign policy, there is a fundamental need for analysts who combine the strongest powers of abstract analysis and philosophical maturity with the direct experience which alone can give a "feel" for the living reality in the making of foreign policy. Too many approaches in the past have been like that of the blind men to the elephant because of their specialization, or their mere lack of imagination and broad experience. In this matter it is clear that the research of the more highly specialized scholars is of extremely limited use except to provide "bricks and mortar" whose arrangement and interpretation then become a job for the broadest and most experienced minds in this field.

In our view it is important to recognize the limitations of the uncritical interdisciplinary approach, which can easily degenerate into a "cross-sterilization" of the social sciences. It is too frequently a matter of record that the mere juxtaposition of a sociologist, an anthropologist, a humanist, a philosopher, a historian, a political scientist, and an economist produces a broth that obviously suffers from too many cooks. All these disciplines have much to contribute, but their contribution must be blended through the interpretive ability of a well-balanced and well-furnished mind.

The organization and control of United States foreign policy is a subject that cannot be comprehended by studies that merely patch together a series of academic specialties. This subject is, for Americans, the practical and operative aspect of the twentieth-century crisis of civilization. It can be dealt with, in all its breadth, only by scholars whose interests range from the fundamental philosophy of human nature to the intricate questions of scientific method and the humdrum technicalities of administrative procedure. Any scholar may well be intimidated by so wide a range and may wish to retreat to a narrower and more manageable field. But scholarship should be willing to tackle the problems that must be dealt with every day by diplomats and soldiers, administrators and Congressmen. Indeed, the scholars who have had some grounding in real political and administrative experience may together provide the skilled insights and the maturity of judgment that is required for the study of our problem. Some such combination may be needed to produce the quality of active interpretation that is characterized by Shakespeare's phrase, "ripeness is all."

AREAS FOR FUTURE STUDY

What, then, are the main areas for future study in this field? Let us summarize them in outline form.

I. IDEAS AND POLITICAL INSTITUTIONS

A. *A Philosophy of Human Nature and Its Relation to Institutions*

(1) More study is needed of the relationship of moral philosophy to the framework of foreign policy, and to foreign policy itself. The nature of man, of course, is a problem that requires unusual insight and powers of integration. The theory of man (in the theological sense) is relevant to the political structure and the foreign policy that we will need for the next half century, and so is all the knowledge that the behavioral sciences can give us. What lessons can we learn from either— or both—regarding the type of political institutions that must be developed by the United States?

(2) History itself—written history—has had an important role in shaping our conceptions of foreign policy. We need only to recall such phrases as "manifest destiny," or the names of Mahan, Beard, and Millis to illustrate the point. We need to know more about the effect of written history on popular conceptions of foreign policy, and on legislative and executive views. And we need historians who are more conscious of their own assumptions.

(3) How much are the ideals and value judgments that determine our foreign policy in harmony with our long-range ideals and interests; and how much are they determined by transitory aspects of our culture, or by overemphasis on past doctrines or events? We may illustrate the importance of this

problem by recalling such slogans as "Freedom of the Seas," or "The Merchants of Death." A study of this problem would lead us into the conceptions that have been held, at one time and another, of our foreign policy and its function in our national life, and in the relation of our nation to world affairs.

(4) An area of quite as great importance to the understanding not only of the substance of foreign policy but of the conditions under which it must be made is the impact of the social and ideological dynamics of our time across national boundaries. These forces, which need to be better understood in order to be countered or guided, shape the destinies of our political systems to a degree that must be apparent to any student of our times. Some so-called "realistic" appraisals of politics completely neglect these most explosive factors and talk as if the logistics of pure physical power could contain the genii in the bottle that have been loosed by the revolutionary ideas now contesting for the loyalties of men. In no area is a more careful type of appraisal needed, since political understanding in this field requires imaginative insight as well as the most mature judgment and deep philosophical analysis.

(5) How may we study this general problem? Its importance forces us to reconsider all our academic habits, and our ideas regarding research techniques—the proper use of the scientific method; the relation of quantitative observation to ideal values; and the role of the scientist and scholar in the events which he must study.

B. The American Constitutional and Federal System

(1) The main outlines of the American constitutional system were based on an eighteenth-century estimate of human nature and its potentialities—an estimate that was perhaps more optimistic than that which guided the development, at least in the nineteenth century, of the British constitution, but more

restrained in its optimism than that of the authors of the liberal and parliamentary constitutions of Europe in the late nineteenth and early twentieth century. Whether or not such a generalization is accurate, it is clear that recent trends in our constitutional development, and in scientific theories of the nature of man and society, justify some systematic study of the fundamental theories that should guide the development of our governmental system.

(2) To correct the bias of a great many specialized studies, we need more research that shows how the government as a whole deals with foreign policy. In the past, many writers—even those who were not engaged in proving their arguments for some particular reform—have selected some branch or department of the government for intensive study. As a result of such specialization, it is easy to become a partisan of the Congress, or the Presidency, or some other part of the government, and to neglect its relations with the rest. The best corrective is probably to study each of the stages involved in the handling of any policy, with particular attention to the interaction of all the institutions and agencies involved. A beginning has been made in this direction by a program of case studies in the making of policy decisions. Without such careful studies, it is easy to blame the Congress or the President for shortcomings that are really the fault of our political system—or vice versa. With such studies, it should be possible to analyze our strengths and weaknesses much more precisely.

(3) Several constitutional amendments have been tentatively recommended in this report. (See pages 58–60 and 179–80 above.) More study is needed of the specific problems that led to these proposals, and of the desirability of these particular remedies. Other proposals, too, deserve study.

There are two alternative sets of assumptions that deserve particularly careful scrutiny. They may be basic to any really far-reaching solutions, or productive of frustration:

(a) The first assumption is that it is too difficult to get sweeping constitutional amendment, and that even if this were possible by calling a federal convention, the results would be so unpredictable as to risk a remedy worse than the disease. There has been no really careful analysis of this fundamental assumption, which has been accepted almost as an article of faith by most American political scientists. It certainly deserves extended study, in the light of our political history and of present possibilities.

(b) The opposite extreme assumption is that if sweeping constitutional changes were made, their effects could be predicted and controlled with sufficient certainty to produce all good, rather than very mixed, results. This assumption, too, deserves a more careful analysis than it has ever had in the light of the effects of previous amendments to our Constitution. The known workings of particular mechanisms like that of the British type of parliament in the innovations which have been grafted upon it (for example, Eire and some of the British Dominions) deserve study for light on the same point.

American political science has been singularly lacking in boldness of hypothesis, combined with scrupulous attempts at analysis and evaluation of the existing institutional patterns that are relevant. It has carried the same failings even more markedly in lack of consideration of the effects of basic constitutional changes in our own and in the kindred British systems. Here, again, is a field deserving the highest talents and wisdom.

(4) The relations between our written and our unwritten Constitution needs to be explored. Much has been made recently of "informal organization," and its relation to the formal structure of administration. No one has studied systematically the relations between formal authority and the informal politi-

cal and administrative processes that control our foreign affairs. Without such studies, it is still a very theoretical speculation, for example, whether a formal constitutional amendment is required to improve some aspects of our legislative-executive relations, and whether certain aspects of the President's coordinating power would be strengthened, or actually weakened, by statutory grants of authority. The logic of a case requires application, for a real test. Analyses of past experiments are wanting and are badly needed; though in their absence we must make both such deductions and such inductions as reason and experience suggest.

(5) What circumstances and methods make it possible to amend the Constitution? If a constitutional amendment is desirable, what does our historical experience show to be the best method to bring it about?

C. The Role of the Congress

(1) What, in political theory, should be the function of the Congress in the American constitutional system? Are any of the functions that it now undertakes incompatible with each other, or with the role of a legislature in our constitutional and federal system—or with the role of any legislature in our present complex society? How can we reconcile the obligations of the member of Congress as a member of the majority (or opposition) party with his obligations to his constituents?

(2) Few studies have been made of the coordination of the legislative process. Historical studies of specific congressional committees, and case histories of the handling of important legislation or policy issues in both the Legislative and Executive Branches, would be useful. Can the leadership of the Speaker and majority leaders be strengthened by the granting of more power to the party policy committees, or by an increase in expert staff? Can more problems of common interest be referred from other committees to the Committees on Foreign Affairs

and Foreign Relations? Such questions can be answered only with the help of deeper studies of congressional committees and their relation to each other and to political leadership.

(3) What are the main tools by which the Congress influences or controls foreign policy? How useful have each of them been in the past, and how useful will they be for various purposes in the future, in the light of modern conditions? Congressional resolutions, committee investigations, the approval or rejection of executive appointments, and the control of appropriations—all have been used in the past, in addition to the ratification of treaties, to exert congressional influence over foreign policy. What are the proper uses and abuses of each method? The appropriations process especially deserves study, in view of the checks and balances that exist between the appropriations committees and other committees of the Congress.

D. The Presidency and the Executive Branch

(1) How are the President's foreign policy decisions influenced or facilitated by party and congressional leaders, and by his executive subordinates? One of the President's main problems is how to organize the Executive Branch so as to tie together the military, the diplomatic, and the economic aspects of foreign policy. We know too little about the work of such coordinating devices as the National Security Council and the International Security Affairs Committee or the Harriman Office. What are the advantages and disadvantages of the formal statutory committee and the less formal interdepartmental committee, and how are both related to the President's Executive Office, and to his ability to make vigorous and judicious decisions? Can the National Security Council be broadened so as to take into account more adequately the economic factors in foreign policy? And what is the relation of a presidential

advisory council (like the Cabinet or the NSC) to the Congress and its committees?

(2) Closely related to the problem of the National Security Council is that of the Department of Defense and the Joint Chiefs of Staff. Problems of military organization have so far been studied mainly by military experts, but the new form of organization in the Department of Defense, and the new role in national and foreign policy that has been given to a military council—the Joint Chiefs of Staff—warrants careful study by other scholars as well. The limits of civilian executive authority over the Joint Chiefs, their relation to the Congress and its committees and to the public, the role of the Secretary of Defense and the three service Secretaries—all these problems are significant to the basic issue of civilian control over our foreign policy. What, for example, are the formal and informal rules governing the congressional testimony of a military officer?

(3) Similarly, we need to know more about the nature of staff work, and its relation to political leadership and executive authority. The judgment of a President or a department head is no longer merely an individual matter; it depends on the way in which his staff work is organized, and the procedures by which it operates. We need to know more about the political and administrative effects of the various ways in which civilian and military staff work are organized.

(4) Since a President can manage the Executive Branch only, controlling central policies and delegating extensive authority to operating agencies, it would be useful to appraise the criteria by which policy and operations may be distinguished in foreign affairs. How can the difference between them be defined? What sanctions can be used to require the operating official to comply with policy decisions? What political forces limit or nullify the effect of such sanctions?

(5) The ambassador in charge of a mission, and the theater commander in charge of the armed forces in an area abroad, are responsible for a range of actions and decisions far broader than the jurisdiction of any single department in Washington. More study is needed of the way in which such an official coordinates the various activities within his area, and in which he is guided and held responsible by his superiors.

II. SOME PROBLEMS IN DEMOCRATIC CONTROL

A. *Parties and Pressure Groups*

American thinking has always been ambiguous about the role of party responsibility in public policy, even though the party and the pressure group have been extensively studied in recent years. Some searching questions still need to be asked, and to be answered by thorough research, regarding the organization of influence over our foreign policy. In what ways is it useful to have unofficial groups organize to influence or control the formal machinery of government, and what limits must be set on them to prevent them from threatening the integrity of public policy?

(1) What is the proper role of partisanship in foreign policy, on what kind of issues should Congress act in a non-partisan manner, and how can the two be distinguished? Closely related, of course, are these questions: What is the responsibility of the opposition party; how is party discipline enforced in each party; to what extent, and by what channels, may the Congress be consulted in the formulation of foreign policy—especially when bipartisan agreement is desired? Future answers to these questions could be made more wisely if we knew more about our past experience and the methods that have worked well, or poorly, under various circumstances.

(2) Domestic pressure groups have a great influence on our foreign policy. Much more should be known about how they

organize support, and how they cooperate with congressional and executive agencies. Among the groups in question are such obvious economic interests as (a) the farm bloc—note, for example, the history of our relations with Argentina; (b) the mine owners—note the silver policy and opposition in building up stockpiles from abroad in peacetime; (c) organized labor; (d) the export-import and shipping interests; (e) groups associated with military policy, such as the American Legion or the Navy League; (f) church and religious groups; (g) special organizations created to deal with foreign affairs, such as the Foreign Policy Association or the Committee to Defend America by Aiding the Allies, or the Council for Prevention of War, or communist front organizations.

(3) The loose coordination of our governmental system has made it possible for foreign governments and foreign nationality groups to exercise great influence at various periods in our history. We need a comprehensive account of the attempts of representatives of foreign governments to influence decisions of the Congress and the Executive—from the time of Citizen Genêt up to the recent consideration of our policy on Spain, China, Israel, and Eire. Sometimes connected with the activities of foreign governments are those of foreign nationality groups and the foreign language press within the United States. Such studies of this problem as those begun by the Office of Strategic Services should be carried on under private auspices.

B. The Press and Public Opinion

(1) The press is more than a neutral mirror of opinion, but we know very little about the way in which various sections of the press further various foreign policies, and the motives for which they do so. The role of the press in such historical incidents as the Spanish-American War is relatively well known, but its part in more recent issues of foreign policy needs more extensive analysis.

(2) Studies should be made of the dynamic effect of press relations on the coordination of foreign policy within the government. The press conference and the "inspired leak" have become essentials of our constitutional procedure. The nature of our libel laws and the lack of discipline with respect to official secrets (in both the Congress and the Executive Branch) have a determining effect on the President's degree of control of the Executive Branch.

C. Politicians and Professionals.

Leaving the professional military service aside for the moment, we need to know more about the roles and relationships of political leaders—especially those in positions of executive authority—and career professionals. What are the motives and ambitions that tend to develop in the two types of careers, and how can they be used for the benefit of society?

(1) We do not know much about the composition of our Foreign Service at various stages in its history. From what social classes and geographic regions did they come, and what was their training and experience? What picture did the Congress and the public have of our foreign service personnel? How was the Foreign Service as a formal corps created? What has been the theory of its relation to political authorities, and to the rest of the government, and how is that theory being modified by current developments?

(2) The nature of public service careers clearly has a great influence on the process of formulating policy. No study has made an adequate appraisal of the advantages and disadvantages of the United States civil service system, which permits entrance at any level in the hierarchy, by comparison with the closed career system. What advantage does the United States system have in preventing the growth of a closed bureaucracy and in making flexible changes in policy possible? How important are its disadvantages in weakening discipline and coordi-

nation? Such questions need to be asked not only of the regular civil service system, but of the use of "dollar-a-year" men and their current counterparts, and of the use of private corporations to carry out public policy under contract (as, for example, in the Atomic Energy Commission program). On the other hand, we need more penetrating studies of the "political" appointments in departments dealing with foreign policy— how much they are influenced by partisan considerations and what contribution they make to the development of policy and the administration of their agencies.

III. POWER, PRINCIPLE, AND POLICY

Three broad issues are worth particular attention in future research on the organization and control of foreign policy: the balance between security and freedom, the role of the military in foreign policy, and the participation of the United States in international organizations.

A. *Security and Freedom*

To consider the current efforts to determine the loyalty of public officials, or to protect the internal security of the nation, it is again necessary for our society to consider what types of ideas may be tolerated in public officials or private citizens, and what methods can be used to enforce compliance and prevent dangerous thoughts or actions without doing more harm than good.

(1) What has been the effect of our loyalty and security enforcement programs (both legislative and executive) on the ability of the United States to conduct its foreign affairs? How effectively, on the one hand, have these programs controlled subversion and espionage? On the other hand, what effect have they had on the development of the public service, and on the morale and efficiency of its members? Finally, what effect have they had on the attitudes of the American people

toward their government, and to the constitutional principles on which it is founded? Some studies have been made in this area, but much more needs to be done to explore the basic issues of justice, freedom, and loyalty as they are applied through administrative and judicial procedures.

(2) Security measures, moreover, have direct effects on our relations with other nations. Our immigration policy, especially in such new manifestations as the McCarran Act, and the control of foreign visitors to the United States presumably have direct and indirect effects on the attitudes of other countries to the United States.

B. The Role of the Military in Foreign Policy

(1) The theory of the use of force in connection with policy —the fundamental relationship between power and principle —deserves study by all possible methods. We must not be content with either the purely military or geopolitical approach at one extreme, or the "one world" approach at the other. What are the circumstances under which force should be used in support of policy or principle? To what extent is military power to be directed to the ends of purely national policy, or to be used in support of principles that transcend national purposes? How may it be controlled so that it will not develop a purpose and political influence of its own beyond control by democratic processes? Studies of the structure of public opinion on all these issues—and their various aspects—would be useful.

(2) The comparative neglect of these topics by historians makes it desirable to study them in historical perspective. The use of armed force without a declaration of war, for example, should be studied, especially in the various crisis periods in American history. Moreover, we need historical studies of the large number of issues in which politics and military considerations interact—grand and campaign strategy, military govern-

ment, industrial mobilization, the politics of soldiers, and the military careers of politicians. The experience of World War II, which has been extensively documented by the specialists and the memoir writers, needs rounded study—especially those undertakings that involved a variety of political and military purposes, such as our policy toward Free France or toward occupied areas.

(3) The vexed issue of what are the proper limits of professional military opinion and competence in the formation of national policy, particularly foreign policy, involve the total concept and organization of civilian control over the military. Our studies indicate that this cannot be settled by a simple cliché. There is a necessarily enlarged and increased area where professional military competence must be given its due weight in the decision-making process and must be protected in its right to express relevant opinions. On the other hand, there is a very serious question always present within the military departments as to how effective the offices of their civilian Secretaries can be in controlling decisions whose details must necessarily be the province and special competence of professionals.

The organization of the military forces themselves pose questions as to the nature and limits of the functions of the Joint Chiefs of Staff. These have the most important bearing on the economic burdens as well as the security and perhaps the survival of the nation. Relations of the professional services to Congress emerge with new importance. How much direct contact between career officers and Congress is appropriate; what sort of testimony may be demanded without endangering national security or undermining civilian control of the executive department over the military—these problems have been dramatically brought to the attention of the public through a series of incidents of the past year or so, noted in our study. Further research of significance lies in analyzing the kinds of control Congress attempts to impose on purely military budgets in a broad sense, that is, in terms of a balanced program.

(4) We have touched on the formal relation of the military services to political authorities within the organization of the Executive Branch, but there are even more important aspects of the role of the career military officer to policy questions. How do his training, the procedure within which he is accustomed to work, and the institutional motives of the service affect his judgment on policy issues? Case studies of the process of decision and action in the field of force and policy are very badly needed. They should be made with a wide angle of observation, for this is not a problem of formal channels of communication but of men in action.

(5) The various relationships between the government and the public on questions of armed force and public policy require much more study. What are the basic attitudes of the civilian public to the military services, both reserve and regular forces? And what is the attitude of the career officer to the politician and to civilian officials? It would be significant to study the kind of attitude expressed by the press and by various groups to certain types of military actions, to certain types of ideas and opinions expressed by military men, or to political activity by officers or ex-officers. The necessary expansion of the military services makes it particularly important to know whatever will help us adjust the role of the armed forces in the political and social system.

C. *International Organization and Multilateral Diplomacy*

Is the nation-state the ultimate form of political organization, or should people hope ultimately to organize the whole world under the rule of law? *How* do we break down these questions, ultimate in character, for manageable and fruitful analysis?

Is there an intermediate stage which under present world

conditions affords an opportunity for organizing the free nations in groups like the North Atlantic Treaty Organization,
or, in more intimate terms, through a union of Europe, or a
North Atlantic Community such as that advocated by those
who support Federal Union? Or are these intermediate stages
fundamentally incompatible with the basic needs of supporting
a United Nations organization or the more sweeping and less
realistic proposals of the World Federalists? How can we
handle even this level of the problems raised, real as their
implications are for the future of our foreign policy?

Even in less ultimate terms, however, we need to examine
with great care the practical possibilities (and limitations on
the possibilities) of national participation in international
organizations.

(1) The relation of the United Nations and other international organizations to the whole structure of law and public
opinion in the United States (and in other countries) needs
careful analysis. To what extent have international organizations, and the principles on which they are based, attracted
a kind of loyalty of their own, both among their staff members
and the general public? To what extent does the support of
public opinion for international organization affect the course
of action of political leaders or diplomats? What has been the
course of public opinion in the United States with respect to
the issues of international cooperation as against isolationism;
how has the traditional attitude of Americans to constitutional
principles influenced their attitude toward the United Nations?
Then, too, how is the work of international organization related
to the legal systems of various countries? Such subjects as
human rights, immigration, and public lands policies—traditionally considered matters of domestic concern—are now important aspects of foreign affairs in which the actions of
judicial bodies are important. The effects of the constitutional

law of various countries on international law, and vice versa, needs thorough study.

(2) We need to organize and evaluate what we know about the effect of multilateral diplomacy—the business of negotiating through international organizations—on the techniques of international relations. We could analyze, for example, the experience of our representatives on the United Nations bodies: what had been the ideological content, for example, of our position in various situations in the United Nations, by comparison with that of our diplomatic action through other channels—and, if there is an important difference, what is the reason for it? Or we could get a clearer idea of the complexity of international organization by analyzing the agenda of various multilateral organizations, comparing them with each other and with the types of problems handled through bilateral channels, examining the roles played by home officers and field staffs in the making of decisions, and comparing the criteria of decision in each case. It would be significant, too, to consider the system of negotiations in which foreign ministers are personally involved: what are the demands which this method places on the time and energy of high officials, how tolerable are those demands to officials in various political or constitutional systems, and what are the effects of such negotiation on other channels of diplomatic business?

(3) Some international organizations, of course, are forums for negotiation, others have more or less power to act, or to administer programs of their own. Not enough study has been given to the practical problems of operating under the authority of a group of nations, or to the way in which different degrees of operating authority require different forms of organization in international agencies. The North Atlantic Treaty Organization will involve problems of command, discipline, and morale that should be compared with the experience of World War II. The International Refugee Organization or the

World Bank or the World Health Organization would bring up similar problems in quite different settings. Each should be studied, not only to see how suitable it is as an instrument of action, but also to see what effect its form or organization has on the national governments concerned and on private groups and general public opinion.

(4) What effect do the various constitutional and administrative systems of different nations have on their respective methods of working with international organizations? Is there any difference, for example, between federal and unitary governments, or between presidential and cabinet systems (to say nothing of democracies and dictatorships) with respect to their ability to cooperate effectively with other nations through multilateral channels?

(5) What light can students of politics throw on the kinds of political organization that fit possible areas of community through various stages of federalism? Is there a definitive limit which can be set to the acceptance of equality of representation on the basis of mere population as between areas of different cultural levels? Some such principle of differential has been accepted in the past, for example, in the Council of the League of Nations and in the Security Council of the United Nations. How much does the doctrine of equality of voting for states large and small in the Assembly add to the prospects of sound international organization, or, on the other hand, involve danger and needless difficulties? Finally, what light can political scientists throw upon the point at which communities become ripe for federal union that would have a bearing on the prospects of European Union, or for Atlantic Union, or for some closer integration for the free countries of the Pacific? Are there any predictive factors in the nature of political community which set limits to such an evolution, or which make it more possible?

Such studies are not merely historical, but they derive a

deepened perspective in the light of history. To plan for security through uniting against aggression, against the centrifugal pulls of nationalism and divergent interests, may be again a principal task of statesmanship in the modern world to which scholarship could lend important aid.

II: PERSONAL COMMENTS OF MEMBERS

OF THE STUDY GROUP

PERSONAL COMMENT OF WILLIAM YANDELL ELLIOTT

A GROUP STUDY involves the dangers of trying to reach a common denominator by watering down real issues, failing to sharpen and strengthen the formulations of either agreements or differences on policies where compromise would be the easier way.

The Preface by the President of the Woodrow Wilson Foundation has indicated our efforts to avoid a document that would be so blurred in its outlines by compromises on details of drafting as to be of little use to our prime purpose: the stimulation of further study of the issues involved.

I should like to express my own appreciation for the spirit in which my colleagues in the Study Group approached the difficult and arduous problem of searching out common ground where possible, and of stating their legitimate differences in the most reasonable spirit for reaching fruitful results. We met for about a day every month and occasionally for extra sessions with some of the distinguished group of consultants named in the Preface by the President of the Woodrow Wilson Foundation. The Study which we are finally printing seems unconscionably long in relation to our originally very modest objectives. It represents, however, a very much boiled down and summary statement redrafted from monographs on separate sections by each member of the group, in the light of an exchange of opinion on many drafts, including the minutes of our discussions.

Only a deep feeling (that I am sure was shared by each of a group of very busy people) could have insured such painstaking efforts: this was the feeling that the result became more worthwhile to each of us in his own thinking the more we worked together. We hope that the final outcome will seem equally worthwhile to others

It naturally fell to my lot as Chairman of the Study Group to do the greater part of the drafting. I have, it follows, less excuse for disagreeing with the Report's formulations than any other member. But just because I have sought to reflect consensus where possible in the drafting and to avoid stating what were only my own views, I may be permitted to point out some issues where a personal emphasis would have differed from that of this group statement.

The first is a comment on the Report's formulation of what constitutes the nature and the limits of possible morality for a nation in our times. In the interest of group expression, the tone of the Report has emphasized less than I should have wished a very basic issue: We all agreed that democracy must combine in its foreign policy a hard core—the morality of freedom—with a realism that does not neglect the traditional aspects of diplomacy or of necessary power. For myself, I should wish personally to go beyond that agreement into substantive issues perhaps not appropriate to this joint report. This is because I believe that procedural devices and processes must depend on how far substantive policies are or should be matters for public support on moral issues that involve men's deepest loyalties. Of course if foreign policies are merely matters for skillful arrangement between professional diplomats, like a well-played game of chess with units of force as the chessmen on the board, this is all nonsense. The whole democratic procedure is at best a nuisance and at the worst a disaster.

More boldly than we have in the text, I should like to stress the necessity of accepting the decision that Woodrow Wilson himself made in challenging superficial conceptions of national interest and settlements by professional diplomacy in these terms. Wilson divined the value to a true national interest of creating some bonds of a responsibly shared effort for a free world. For this moral community among nations, freedom and self-determination were the essential bases. His League was to be a League of free states. It was not merely accidental that the first mortal stroke to the League came from Japan, which had been a doubtful member from this definition, and that the *coup de grace* came at the hands of the dictators. Today we have set up a world forum that has compromised that issue in the hope of persuading Moscow to peace by compromise— so far by concession. That road has led us through painful stages of disillusionment, to NATO and to post-Korean War rearmament.

Indeed it leads us perhaps to reexamine our past wishful thinking and to beware of those apostles of settlements through appeasement who parade a tough "realism" based on a calculus of power in the so-called "national interest." The trouble with such formulae is that they overlook that men's moral loyalties are often the most important ingredient of real power. Future adherents to the United Nations, if we are not to destroy that organization's moral claim to speak for peoples, ought to be admitted only if they are really free nations. Nor should the Western powers ever concede the *legality* of Soviet control over liberated countries behind the Iron Curtain where elections are not really free, as was promised in the provisional peace settlements at the end of World War II. We cannot press this issue to a showdown today for lack of strength. But we should never deceive ourselves that we have ultimately gained strength if we concede to Moscow the legal and final right to enslave other nations with even our tacit consent.

The text of this Report has noted that the incorporation of free elections and the principle of self-determination for peoples (to the latter of which Lenin himself paid repeated lip service) have to be realistically modified in terms of the relative maturity of states by Wilson's concept of "trusteeship" under some form of international mandate (see page 22). Really undeveloped and politically immature peoples are not ready for the responsibilities of self-government and international full partnership. But the essential point to emphasize (it seems to me more than we have in the Report) is that nothing is gained by concessions to Moscow that involve a genuine surrender of principles which are basic to any hopes of permanent peace. We cannot even buy time that Moscow does not in any case need to concede. This applies to the surrender of the principle of free elections in countries liberated from the Nazi yoke, including Germany. Indeed, it applies with quite as much force and with undoubtedly as much importance to the future unity and strength of the free world as does the now clearly recognized necessity for having an inspection of Soviet armed strength, including atomic weapons, as a necessary concomitant to promises of disarmament. Settlements that surrender a basic principle are never settements. They produce the conditions of further surrender and sow confusion and despair and the conditions for a world explosion in much the way that Munich did prior to World War II.

A second difference in emphasis rises from consideration of the question, "How much constitutional reform and when?"

The degree to which this representative and, I dare say, high-level group did agree on some basic amendments to our Federal Constitution as necessary to the better and more stable conduct of our foreign policy was of course most gratifying to me. After all, as a "Constitutional Reformer" of long standing, I have perhaps (along with Mr. Thomas K. Finletter, *et al.*) a sort of "vested interest" in this view! But it is my personal conviction that there is a considerable danger—greater than is indicated in the Report—that the pressure for survival in the deadly struggle with the Soviet system, if it is not more adequately met, may force us into Caesarism. This double danger of defeat or loss of freedom (which is unified by the weakness of our pressure-ridden system for meeting a long-sustained period of crisis involving national survival) seems to me peculiarly great today. It will remain true, in my view, so long as our intellectual and political leaders tend to treat constitutional reform as either impossible, or unnecessary, or dangerous, or of such remote interest as to be put off until the Greek Kalends—that is, to some time when we have satisfactorily finished off all the other more pressing and immediate issues. That this latter attitude is a characteristic of human nature and not peculiar to our system, I admit. But I submit that to put off reforms, even when accepted as desirable, has become a peculiarly rooted characteristic of our system, partly because of the very success of the men of 1787, who established so admirable a Constitution that it has become an object of veneration. This veneration extends to its mechanics, as well as to its spirit. Yet the mechanics of a political system suitable to an eighteenth-century agrarian setting may simply not fit the needs of the latter half of the twentieth century.

As to the present working of our political mechanics, it is my own conviction that no amount of mere exhortation to increase party discipline and responsibility has very much chance of success. You can't "educate" Congress against the grain of political habits rooted in the necessity of getting elected under the present system. The only way in which Congress is going to be persuaded to change its present methods of scrutinizing the details of executive policy and trying to change policy by blocking or intimidating certain types of its exercise is to get an effective way of forcing a broader alignment of executive policy with a program to which the dominant party in Congress is committed also—that is, by a general election. Only basic constitutional changes would produce the necessary unification of responsibility. The simple method for bringing about more party responsibility would be to introduce an opportunity for breaking a deadlock between the President and Congress. This can be done by a constitutional amendment which would allow the Chief Executive *once* during his four-year term the right of appeal to the electorate, *if he so chooses,* by calling a general election, involving at least the seats of the House of Representatives. I should, today, be willing to add the corollary: a President who lost such a test should immediately resign and have his successor (chosen by joint balloting of the two houses in a joint session of the new Congress) become President until the next regular four-year term election. This would break deadlocks.

Such a proposal, though sweeping, is only a partial approach to the parliamentary system of Canada, our close federal neighbor, with problems of minorities and of local differences as great as our own, where the full-fledged parliamentary system itself works with remarkable success. It does not destroy our judicial review or other checks and balances, nor impose the rigidities of the full ministerial responsibility of the British system.

Since I advocated the sort of changes just outlined in *The Need for Constitutional Reform* (published in the early days of the New Deal in 1935), I have not altered my view that it was *not* necessary to have the President's Cabinet chosen from those who had won seats in such a general election, in the British or Canadian manner. I have, however, come to the conclusion that the fruits of victory in a general election ought to carry with them added weight in Congress, again by a constitutional amendment which would assure that at least ten principal members of the President's Cabinet (who were *chosen by him*, but subject to ratification by the Senate in the usual way) should have the right both to sit and to vote in the Senate; and the corresponding right of twenty of the members of his Cabinet or heads of agencies, chosen at his discretion, to sit and vote in the House of Representatives. This would make victory at any general election carry with it voting power to put into effect a party program. The Study Group limited its approval of this notion to a very broad endorsement of this general direction, with the natural reservation that, since the idea developed late in our discussions, it was too new to them to be fully analyzed in the time at our disposal.

Such a position for members of the Cabinet, I should myself urge, would not only strengthen the President's hold on Congress and its policies and make the contest for a general election decisive for national policy; it would also and more effectively than any of the other suggestions known to me (for example, having Cabinet members merely answer questions or combine with Congress in joint legislative-executive councils) tend to bridge the appalling gap that exists between the two ends of Pennsylvania Avenue—the White House and the Capitol. That it would have an important bearing on the choice of Cabinet members is possible. But that it would lower the standard of the executive or the legislative performance I cannot believe possible or probable. It would certainly offer some hope of establishing a more cooperative relationship and better channels of information than the present seniority-ridden committee system affords, as well as more effective party discipline and program control, which democracy so badly requires in times of crisis.

For quiet and more sheltered times our over-checked and too much balanced system might well continue to serve, in spite of its manifest encouragement of government by pressure, rather than government in the public interest. No government can approach perfection except in some philosopher's utopia. But a long practice and personal experience of the frustrations of policy formation and some acquaintance with the necessary resulting technique of evasion and guerrilla warfare between the two branches, as well as with the proneness to duck difficult issues rather than to face them, leads me to the conclusion that ours is not the best possible government, certainly not the best possible for what is not on any account the best of possible worlds—somewhat to turn to my purpose a paraphrase of the optimism of Leibnitz.

Perhaps this will indicate sufficiently a line of emphasis which I would on my own responsibility alone have strengthened in the presentation of our study. It may perhaps also betray a temper that some will feel lacks that quiet patience related to the acceptance of the "historical sweep of things." It may be that I can be detected in this as overemphasizing the immediacy and the peril of our national crisis, and that this tendency has strongly affected my predilection for seeking basic solutions and bolder policies. Most of the points of disagreement that follow in the personal statements of the other members arise from a feeling that where I have stated alternatives I have sometimes argued one better than the other. But I should like to point out that they are stated as alternatives and that the case for the more orthodox view is in no danger of going without champions. I am glad that one or two of my colleagues have added a word of personal comment to be sure that moderation and caution have their due.

As to the ultimate test of who is divining more nearly the shape of things to come, heaven grant that *they* may be more right than my devil's advocate! Such a judgment must await the outcome of the immediate years ahead for a short-term answer. And who can forecast accurately the judgment of history? Even history has its secular swings of fashions and its periodical conflicts of schools. We must, after all, live by such light as we can gain from the past in facing the future, according to our basic values. If we surrender those, how shall we keep our own hearts tempered to stern times? And how raise a worthy standard for the adherence of others? Nations which have lost their essential *characters* can no more than individuals offer a way of hope, worth sacrifice, to others. Patching up machinery cannot cover up such a loss. But failure to get the right kind of machinery may make the loss inevitable.

Our inquiry would seem to me to show that it is never when our national leadership has been true to the deepest moral insights of *responsible* freedom that we have failed or tragically blundered. We have been strongest, both at home and abroad, precisely when we stuck to morals and not moralizing, at the same time remembering that inner conviction is the base of all morale, and consequently of force which can meet a real challenge or testing.

Nor is this, in my own judgment, too far away from the true insights of one of our greatest leaders who also strove to understand how better to control and organize our foreign policy. That Woodrow Wilson should have run the gamut of Secretaries of State from Bryan, the western crusader for perfection and peace here and now, to the somewhat narrow technical professionalism of Lansing shows the range of possible emphasis on the problem we have discussed. That he should have tempered the skill and sometimes prophetic insight of his personal adviser Colonel House with his own sense of moral and political realities is no more than is expected and necessary of the Chief Executive, who as political leader of this country must accept final responsibility. But most of all, his failure lay as much in losing his hold on Congress and the country as in any failure to utilize negotiating talents. The two things went hand-in-hand. Great leadership is not just magical or charismatic. It must take full advantage of opportunities for unifying forces where they exist (bipartisan support) and organize the basis for strength at home in order to have any weight abroad. It must be able to compromise where compromise will promote, not destroy, moral consensus.

What, after all, is the possibility of political leadership? Is it affected by the mechanics of its political system? Can France, for example, produce a steady leader under the sort of parliamentarianism and electoral system in present operation?

In the end, no man can far transcend the understanding or reach of the people whom he represents. He may lift them as he himself is lifted up. But he may be broken by the pull of that mass weight when he drags it, reluctant, to the trial. The public must be committed by a previous education as to the true issues and their import. Here party discipline and responsibility help to educate support. The greatest advantage of a general election with the presidency at stake is that it focuses nation-wide interest on the issues involved. It helps to create, promote, and make effective a real national consensus for more political responsibility.

Our machinery permits this, but it adds a great element of risk and irrelevance by mid-term elections. Furthermore, a retiring President, or one who has lost his hold on Congress, can only sulk in silence or stand painfully on his dignity until his term of humiliation expires. If a more responsible support is needed, with public education and a "commitment" by the nation, why should not the possibility of a general election to break deadlocks take the place of our "off-year" elections? I urge that this would simplify party responsibility, strengthen the Executive without Caesarism, and make possible a stronger moral stand because the strengths and limits of national support would be clear. Foreigners are prone to misjudge our policy and its results because our peculiar system increases the impression of weakness beyond any reality. There are good grounds for believing that hostilities in the twentieth century have sprung from such misconceptions of our real policy and our strength.

PERSONAL COMMENT OF McGEORGE BUNDY

Differences within our Group have shaped themselves increasingly as matters of degree, not kind; and I shall take only a few lines to define without defending my own general emphases, within the framework set forth in the Chairman's Report.

I accept the logic which leads to proposals for constitutional reform, but I am not inclined to be hopeful about the prospects for their early acceptance; while at the same time I am not certain that they would be as helpful as the Chairman's language sometimes implies. I am impressed with that part of our agreed analysis which traces our difficulties to sources deeper than our constitutional system. Yet if time and place should offer, I would strongly support a practical effort to move in the direction the Report's proposals indicate.

Within the existing constitutional pattern, I am inclined to look for improvement in two areas—the temper and attitude of the American people and the organization and leadership of the Executive Branch. I think it likely that many of the disturbances and failures of recent years are a part of the pains of a national adjustment to a wholly new relationship to the world. This adjustment has been as marked for the professional diplomat or soldier as for the most insulated private citizen, and on the whole I am more impressed with the distance we have come than with the distance we have still to travel.

Progress has also been registered in executive leadership and administration. But here I am impressed by the amount that remains to be done, and that can be done, whenever there is a sufficient skill and understanding in the White House and the Cabinet. I therefore subscribe with particular force to those parts of the Report which emphasize the great roles and opportunities of the President, the Secretary of State, and the Secretary of Defense. I am much drawn by the historian's view that the Executive is the usual instrument of great new developments, and I see the problem of administration as one of setting free and supporting the forces which make for active leadership on the highest level. This leadership I see as political in three senses of the word—in its continuing connection with national opinion, in its insistence that high policy includes and subsumes the military and strategic elements of action, and in its assertion that professional diplomacy, while a great instrument, can never be the master of the national purpose. I recognize the weight which this emphasis places on the character of individuals, and especially the character of the President of the United States. I can only say that I think the emphasis accurate. As a specific example of my difference with the Chairman on this point, I would suggest that Mr. Truman's policy of military economy before Korea was a policy which Mr. Truman could quite easily have changed by the use of his own office and powers. I think this episode shows inadequate leadership, not the power of pressure groups.

I must also enter a reservation as to the tone of the discussion on pages 216–18. As to the central point, that assumptions as to the urgency of any given problem affect judgments on the adequacy of our machinery for dealing with it, there can be no disagreement. Yet it seems to me that this part of the Chairman's Report, if only by stating one of the alternatives with such vigor, gives more weight to certain apocalyptic possibilities than the balance of the Study Group opinion would justify. I cannot resist the further suggestion that if it be true that time is not on our side, I do not see how we can afford to take the time that would be needed to work for constitutional reform. This alternative hypothesis, if adopted, would, in short, cut very deep in respect to many policies. It should be and properly is pointed out as an important alternative. My feeling is that our national policy, generally supported by the Study Group, has correctly rejected this hypothesis, at least for the present.

But in the main I would emphasize our agreements and not our differences. The student of American foreign policy can never become expert in more than a few matters, and he must continually be impressed by the contingent and fragmentary character of the materials from which he tries to think. For me, as a member of the Study Group, it has been heartening to find that most of my thinking could be connected with the thoughts of men who, taken together, had a wide and deep understanding of many aspects of the matter; and in the process much of what I thought has been modified and I think improved. I think that our discussions have produced, at least for ourselves, an understanding which is larger than the sum of its original parts, and this is not always the way of Group inquiry. So I would say that such value as our work may have is more likely to be found in the Report as a whole than in our individual comments.

PERSONAL COMMENT OF GEORGE KENNAN

The contribution which the professional servant of government could make to this sort of study has been a limited one. His knowledge of American government outside the Executive Branch was too superficial to permit him to contribute much on this score beyond the vague stirrings that are apt to make themselves felt in the breast of the ordinary uninitiated citizen. Even allowing for the fact that he was on leave of absence, the disciplined nature of his own status vis-a-vis the government inhibited him from commenting on questions of current policy; and he would like now to feel himself and his associates in government uncommitted by such statements and implications concerning substantive policy problems as the Report necessarily had to contain.

His interest centered, accordingly, on three problems on which it seemed to him that his own experience gave him the right to make suggestions. These were:

(A) How could we achieve a deeper, clearer, and more unified concept of national interest, to serve as a foundation for the work of government in the conduct of external relations?

(B) How could government, particularly the Executive Branch, be so streamlined and reordered as to give it a more effective and fluid control over those of its own activities that have important impacts on other countries?

(C) How could our government make better use of professional training and experience in evolving foreign policy and conducting external relations?

With regard to the first of these questions, it seemed to him that there must be a greater recognition of the need for well-thought-through concepts of the national interest in external affairs, and for a unified understanding of these concepts and a disciplined relation to them on the part of all persons concerned with our foreign relations. The plea was not for any intellectual domination along totalitarian lines but merely for a recognition of the fact that in the field of foreign affairs, as in any other, too many cooks can spoil the broth, and that foreign policy which is a chaotic mixture of everybody's ideas is not necessarily good foreign policy.

With respect to the organization of the Executive Branch for the conduct of foreign relations, it seemed to the professional that one of our difficulties as a nation lay in too narrow a view of what constituted foreign relations. We were inclined to think that it was limited to those things the Department of State normally corresponded about with other governments. Actually, it was something much wider: it embraced all forms of behavior of our government and people that produced significant impacts on the lives of other peoples and the interests of other governments. If we were to conduct our foreign relations effectively, one of the prerequisites for doing so would be to gather up all the threads of control over these various manifestations of American public and private life and try to see that they were all manipulated for a unified and intelligible purpose. The professional was perhaps more alarmed than his colleagues by the prospect of a continuation of government by committee meetings, seldom embracing any clear allotment of individual responsibility. As a corrective, he could see only the establishment of some sort of Assistant President, with real authority over all those phases of government operation, including defense, that represented part of our foreign relations. Whether this was to be achieved by creating a new position in the Executive Office or by making the Secretary of State a real Prime Minister for External Relations (which means in effect a Prime Minister for the broader national interests of our people in general) seemed to him a secondary question compared to the need of getting something like this done somewhere.

With regard to the third of these problems, namely, the use made of people like himself and his associates, the professional could only submit that a good career service in the field of external relations was something that could not be said to have failed, for the simple reason that it had really never been tried with the requisite determination and persistence. In the growing complexity of our international problems and the demands they make on the judgment, competence, and maturity of understanding of the persons involved in foreign relations work, the professional saw the vindication in principle of his own calling, whether or not the public was satisfied with its present devotees as a class. He expressed his conviction that no one could really go through the violent intellectual exercise of living in, attempting to understand, the world outside our borders without finding himself different in certain ways from "folks back home." He entered his plea that people should accept this difference, which had nothing whatsoever to do with loyalty, and not permit it to become a source of undue concern to them or an occasion for the continued ridicule and abuse of the people involved.

In each of these three fields, he saw hopeful possibilities for the attention of the scholar, and was confident that a measured and objective approach to the problem involved could yield rich fruits in the improvement of America's performance as a member of the world community.

PERSONAL COMMENT OF DON K. PRICE*

This is not a dissenting opinion, but a postscript—ideas that, it seems to me, were given too little weight while preparing our Report.

First, I think we should have put more emphasis on this question: which types of legislative control are most effective, and most important for the democratic process? Does Congress do better by trying to maintain a number of detailed controls at once, or would it be more effective if it concentrated its fire on broad policy issues through a smaller number of legislative channels?

Does Congress, for example, control policy more effectively by trying also to pass on the details of administration? Does it control policy more effectively by having separate committees for legislative, appropriation, and investigatory purposes? Is its control of general financial policy strengthened or weakened by having separate committees act on appropriations and on revenues, and by having detailed subcommittee consideration of appropriations for each bureau and department?

* Mr. Price on February 1, 1952, became a staff member of the United States Department of Defense. This statement was written before he returned to government service.

We have to choose in the United States, it seems to me, between the advantages of detailed legislative scrutiny of administration and the advantages of close executive coordination —or we may make some sort of a compromise between the two. Much of the difficulty that we attribute to the separation of powers is really caused by the unwillingness of the Congress to accept or reject policy in a single package, and by its determination to let its own committees and subcommittees make detailed policy decisions even when they contradict each other.

The result is that Congressmen are reluctant to permit any real center of authority on foreign policy to develop within the Executive Branch. They are likely to support or to encourage opposition to the President and the Department of State by other executive agencies. For example, I might quote from the Congressional Record of September 25, 1951, a remark by Congressman Wolcott, who was speaking in praise— yes, in praise—of the Export-Import Bank: "But I will have to admit, and I shall admit, that there is no evidence whatsoever that the Export-Import Bank has ever been used in any instance under pressure of the State Department to further our foreign policy."

As long as this is a typical attitude in the Congress (and perhaps of the public), I do not think the basic problem is whether or not we ought to have a constitutional amendment. Some types of constitutional amendment, it seems to me, would leave us about where we are now, or even make our situation worse. Others might improve our government considerably. But whether or not a constitutional amendment is desirable, it is important in the United States to develop a general consensus that is more favorable to the strengthening of political responsibility in the Congress, and to the coordination of administration by the President; without such a consensus a formal constitutional amendment would be useless, and with such a consensus it might be unnecessary.

I need not go into detail on this point, around which much of the discussion in our Study Group turned, because the Woodrow Wilson Foundation has published a lecture (*The New Dimension of Diplomacy*) in which I set forth my ideas at undue length.

Next, we neglected, I believe, to give as much weight as we should to the important problem of personnel. As Americans, we are all too likely to think that policy can simply be legislated into existence. We rarely give enough weight in public discussion to the question of whether we are making it possible to carry out the policy we have already decided on. This is partly a matter of organization, on which we have made a great deal of progress in recent years, and partly a matter of personnel, on which we have gone backward rapidly.

It is still true that the civil service, by comparison with the military services, cannot provide a planned career for an able executive. It is even more true than it was a decade or two ago that the civilian services generally—the Foreign Service as well as the civil service—have lost a great deal of their attractiveness in spite of the tremendous increase in the scope of their functions and their influence. The causes are fairly obvious: partly a matter of material reward, but even more a matter of lack of public esteem, and lack of protection against unwarranted political attack. When a Secretary of State reports, as he recently did, that only half as many young men had applied for foreign service examinations as during the previous year, we may make a rough estimate of the damage that irresponsible Congressional attacks in 1950 will have done to the quality of American diplomacy in 1980.

The effects of this influence all aspects of government. The nature of civil-military relations in the United States, for example, is likely to depend much less on constitutional principle than on the ability of the civilian side of the government to put men of high ability and continuous experience to work on the same broad international questions to which the military services can devote an overwhelming battery of disciplined talent. The civilian side of government cannot do so now. As students of government and foreign affairs, we could select no more fundamental aspect of our problem for emphasis.

PERSONAL COMMENT OF ARTHUR SCHLESINGER, Jr.

As the historian in the Group, I found myself often in the position of deprecating the importance of mechanics and exalting that of politics in tackling the problems with which we were concerned. In the course of the highly instructive discussions, however, I did come to modify the original suspicion with which I had regarded most projects for constitutional reform. Yet constitutional reform plainly can be no cure-all; and, while I agree that governmental structure often frustrates leadership, yet changes in governmental structure, in my judgment, are likely to have only a limited effect in producing the leadership without which any structure will founder. Accordingly, I still feel that political leadership and political education remain the primary—if intangible and elusive—factors which will determine the fate of our foreign policy and nation.

In this connection the ambiguous status of the American President, the customary source and focus of national leadership, requires attention. The President must be both leader of party and leader of country. To reject the party system would be to import a new and sinister element in modern American politics; to surrender to it would be to abdicate the responsibilities of national leadership. A non-party leader would be an indigestible element in a democracy; a leader who could not see beyond party would be inadequate to a national crisis. The great democratic leader therefore must accept his partisan status and then transcend it. In Abraham Lincoln, a man who fused the reflexes of a party politician with the overriding vision of a statesman, we have the classical resolution of this problem. When Woodrow Wilson reverted from statesmanship to party in the congressional elections of 1918, he violated the public image of leadership. Franklin D. Roosevelt's greatest moments were those, at the depth of depression and the height of war, when he spoke to the people as a national, and not as a party, leader; yet, his claim to national leadership was acceptable only because it had emerged from the interplay of partisanship and was subject to its check and discipline.

Our great Presidents—and particularly the two Roosevelts—have had a vivid and explicit conception of politics as, in part, the art of popular education. One main obligation of leadership, they felt, was to raise the general level of public information and understanding. Early in 1934 Franklin D. Roosevelt exulted in what he described as "the amazing and universal increase in the intelligent interest which the people of the United States are taking in the whole subject of government. In cities, in hamlets, and on farms men and women in their daily contacts are discussing, as never before except in time of war, the methods by which community and national problems are ordered." Today, in time of cold war, that educational impulse has receded in our political leadership, until we are faced with the paradox of what is (in my judgment, at least) a wise foreign policy, courageously and intelligently conceived and well understood by those who conceived it, but confusing and obscure to most people in the country. This is not a failure of policy; it is a failure in the communication of policy, a failure in education, in leadership. Nor would structural changes make up for the deficit in leadership.

I would add two specific points:

1) If continued foreign crisis produces a continuing tendency toward the concentration of power in the Executive, then the traditional civil liberties may find their place in

society subtly but profoundly threatened. As the energy of society becomes increasingly centripetal, in other words, the rights of opposition and dissent must be braced as never before if they are not to be swallowed up in the vortex. This means, in my judgment, that if Caesarism is to be avoided, the strengthening of the Executive must be accompanied by ever more explicit and meaningful guarantees for the rights of dissent. It would seem to me that civil liberties should now be regarded as a public interest deserving specific governmental support and protection: in this connection, I would note briefly, as deserving further study, the various proposals to establish some form of "claimant agency" within government for civil liberties—the American Civil Liberties Union's proposal, for example, for a "public defender" to sustain the claims of civil freedom within the government, or Professor Harold Lasswell's suggestion that both Congress and the Executive designate committees or officials charged especially with the protection of individual freedom.

2) I share the feeling expressed by Mr. Bundy that the apocalyptic alternative in the section on "Alternative Assumptions as to the Nature of the Threat and its Timing" (pages 216ff.) is argued so much more cogently than the other as to give an unbalanced impression of the tone of the Group's discussion of this point. I would be among those members of the Group who would feel rather strongly that war is not inevitable, and that our present foreign policy offers in the main a good chance of averting war.

INDEX